Arts and Inspiration

An artist is a seer, a revelator, and a prophet. He, therefore, must be a man of God. He has great power to influence the hearts and minds of men, and great, therefore, is his responsibility. To be an artist requires much faith, hope, belief, devotion, and love.

Anselm Spring

Arts and Inspiration

Mormon Perspectives

Edited by Steven P. Sondrup

Brigham Young University Press

Front cover: "Collage," by Johan H. Benthin

Library of Congress Cataloging in Publication Data

Main entry under title:

Arts and inspiration.

   1. Arts, Mormon–Addresses, essays, lectures.
2. Art and religion–United States–Addresses, essays, lectures. I.
Sondrup, Steven P.
NX663.U5A77   700'.88283   80-2127
ISBN 0-8425-1845-2 (pbk.)

International Standard Book Number: 0-8425-1845-2

Contents

Art and Life

List of Contributors   154

Foreword

The appearance of this book is an important event for the Mormon people. Implicit in these pages is the recognition of the fundamental significance of art in Mormon life. There are, of course, many in this culture who see art primarily as filigree, a kind of entertainment to be indulged only after all the truly important business of family, Church, and profession has been satisfied. There are others, too, who see art as an end itself, not just *an* end, but *the* end, a devotion to which should supersede all other devotions, including family, Church, and profession.

For the understanding Mormon neither position is, of course, correct. And as these essays collected here remind us, there is in the Mormon ethos not just a concern but a certain commitment to that which is "virtuous, lovely, or of good report." To the hardworking sculptor or playwright, that commitment may often seem subdued, if not entirely forgotten. However, it does exist, and, though forgotten by many, it can be rediscovered and revitalized for us at any time by those who have the will, understanding, and faith. In helping make that discovery again, these pages lead us a long way.

Furthermore, the exercise of seeking after these things, of wrestling the critical muses of our own culture as Jacob did his angel, soon persuades us that there is much more to this matter than we might have thought. And as the light dawns, we often discover not a Mormon exclusiveness, but a worldwide association with other children of God who have been touched in their genius by the divine fire. The reasons, certainly, have to do with the unity of all truth and the fact that good art is true. In his *A Guide for the Perplexed,* E. F. Schumacher makes the point clearly that true art is never entirely entertainment nor propaganda.

> All great works of art are "about God" in the sense that they provide a Guide for the Perplexed, such as Dante's *Divine Comedy.* Dante wrote for ordinary men and women, not for people with sufficient private means to be interested mainly in fine feelings. "The whole work," he explains, "was undertaken not for a speculative but a practical end ... the purpose of the whole is to remove those living in this life from a state of misery, and lead them into a state of felicity." ... To treasure art simply for its beauty is to miss the point. The true function of art is "so to dispose [the] heart with desire of going" "up the mountain," *which is what we really wish to do but keep forgetting,* that we "return to our first intent." [pp. 129–31]

It is this intermediary function of art and the necessity of faith that makes the discussion of art so important for Mormons.

In this particular volume we are fortunate to have an editor who understands these relationships so well. Steven Sondrup is well known as a scholar and critic whose apt judgment and enlightened insights make him particularly well qualified to take up the task of this book. This impressive gathering of essays demonstrates better than words how much we owe to the unflagging enterprise of this fine man. He himself modestly suggests that there will yet be much to say about this important topic in other books at other times. But for us, here and now, looking back over one hundred fifty years of Mormon growth, this volume is a landmark of its own from which many will take their bearings for years to come.

Neal E. Lambert
Associate Academic Vice-President
Brigham Young University

Preface

The relationship between religion and art has long been problematic and fraught with difficulties and inconsistencies. On the one hand, some of the most sublime and moving artistic creations have been derived from or inspired by religious considerations and, sometimes, commissioned for religious use. Yet, on the other hand, paintings have been slashed, sculptures smashed, and organs destroyed in the name of religion. Both the form and the content of art have been at once sources of religious inspiration and irritation, and the situation shows little evidence of immediate change: Art and religion remain the most tenuous of friends but the most reluctant of enemies.

Within the Mormon community the same paradox obtains, but without either the positive or the negative extremes evident in the world at large. Beginning, perhaps, with the Lord's admonition to Emma Smith to collect sacred hymns (D&C 25), and continuing through the calling of art missionaries to study painting in France and through various other kinds of direct and indirect support of the arts, the Church has fostered the cultivation of aesthetic sensitivity. Yet, at times, prominent authorities have questioned some of the fundamental assumptions that make art possible. It is clear, though, that on the whole the Church has encouraged the pursuit of artistic expression that is virtuous, lovely, or of good report. Thus, there is ample room for discussion of the ways in which art can make important religious perceptions more profoundly real and spiritually moving and the means by which religious understanding can more effectively inform the creative impulse and give it more than temporal meaning.

Although it would be a thankless task to attempt a definition of *art* or even *Mormon art,* two caveats seem appropriate, the first warning against an all-too-narrow view of what art is and the second cautioning against an excessively broad concept. Too often in matters of religious and aesthetic merit, individuals show themselves to be willing prisoners of social and cultural conditioning: Only familiar items, those that fit perfectly into established conceptual categories, are allowed to speak to the soul. Artistic sensitivity is narrowly confined by past experience and by arbitrary expectations of what may have aesthetic appeal and be of religious significance. Such rigidly circumscribed responsiveness is lamentable, because it limits the potential for experiencing the spiritual joy and intellectual enrichment that art conceived in terms of a wide variety of norms and in extremely varied cultural contexts can afford. Because the Church is based on the principle of continuing revelation, because new truths are being revealed on an ongoing basis, creative artists in the Church must be prepared to communicate new insights in a language that at once is uniquely suited to the needs of the message and at the same time speaks resoundingly to the hearts of men. The artist must be accorded the latitude to make his work as living and vital as the Church itself.

Moreover, as the Church enters ever more dramatically into a cosmopolitan frame of reference, members must be willing not only to accommodate but also to welcome and rejoice in previously unknown and even unimagined ways of praising God, of singing a joyful song, of celebrating the triumph of Christ, of proclaiming the reality of the Restoration. The challenge is clearly not so to restrict artistic expression that the mind can easily understand the results, but rather so to expand the sensitivity of the human spirit that it can encompass the best work of the most inspired artists. While nurturing a willing responsiveness to varied forms of artistic expression, one must also be cautious about assuming that all creative endeavors achieve the degree of excellence that invites appreciation in aesthetic terms. Just as the strained efforts of beginning musicians and the hasty scribbles of the energetic child—commendable though they may be—are not art in the loftiest and most important sense, casual jottings—rhymed though they may be—do not make a poem. The implication of this observation is emphatically not that only the most accomplished should dare to indulge the muse but rather that there is an important difference between essentially private efforts emphasizing aesthetic exploration and openly public performances striving for heightened communication. Art in the best and broadest sense of the word necessarily involves inspiration, vision, or creativity and a mastery of medium, form, and style. The untrained hand cannot make the violin sing no matter how moved it may feel, and the untrained mind cannot unite thought with image or concept with metaphor to create the moving, essentially poetic statement. A soul-searing testimony and profound commitment may render a soul a candidate for salvation, but they alone do not make art.

The guiding principle in organizing this anthology has been the desire to present a wide range of views and judgments that reflect different attitudes, cultures, and arts. The goal was not a unified or systematic analysis of the relationship between Mormon culture and the arts but rather a pluralistic approach that invites later complementary and synthesizing investigations. The essays included in this volume are written from varying perspectives and from within contrasting cultural milieux; they represent many different approaches ranging from abstract, theoretical studies to highly personal statements; the focus of some is unabashedly academic, while others are refreshingly casual. No attempt has been made to minimize or level these differences, because the varied approaches and styles so eloquently attest to the richness and flexibility of the question. Like many anthologies, though, this volume must remain somewhat of a disappointment, not in the least for what it says but rather for what, for practical considerations, had to be left unsaid. Some issues might have been explored in more detail, many other areas might have been investigated; more questions might have been asked, and more answers might have been provided. The essays that are provided, though, are representative, provocative, and informative and raise issues and challenges that invite thoughtful consideration and further investigation.

.The artistic accomplishments of the Church's first one hundred fifty years stand as a worthy heritage: They speak in many voices of sacrifice, hardship, loss, hope, accomplishment, triumph, and joy. They elicit self-satisfaction and pride. But they must not be allowed to suggest indifference or complacency. President Kimball has eloquently described his hope that members of the Church will be able to combine talent, training, and inspiration to produce works of art as ennobling and beautiful as any the world has ever known.

> For years I have been waiting for someone to do justice in recording in song and story and painting and sculpture the Restoration, the reestablishment of the kingdom of God on earth, the struggles and frustrations; the apostasies and inner revolutions and counter-revolutions of those first decades; of the exodus; of the counter-reactions; of the transitions; of the persecution days, of the miracle man, Joseph Smith, of whom we sing "Oh, what rapture filled his bosom, [/] For he saw the living God;" and of the giant colonizer and builder Brigham Young.[1]

The goal has been defined, but the means of fully achieving it are yet to be found. As artists who have shaped their talent by arduous training and have animated it by the light of inspiration come forward bearing works that begin to do justice to the message of the Restoration, members of the Church who are prepared with sensitivity and understanding to accept the gift will be richly rewarded. In striving for perfection—the best and the greatest—neither the giver nor the receiver can be satisfied with mediocrity: Excellence alone repays the blessing of the birthright.

Steven P. Sondrup

1. The Gospel Vision of the Arts," *Ensign* (July 1977), p. 5.

Acknowledgments

Many people have contributed in various ways to the preparation and production of this volume. Financial aid was provided by, among others, the Brigham Young University College of Fine Arts and Communications and the Research Division. Minnie P. Burton, Holger G. Nickel, Brenda Janson, George S. Tate, Maren M. Mouritsen, Marilyn R Miller, Eric Shumway, Larry Shumway, Todd A. Britsch, Ronald Mead Horton, Madison U. Sowell, Teddie Krause, Craig Watts, and Nancy Richards Clark have been most generous in providing diverse kinds of help and encouragement. Elizabeth Wilkinson played a very significant role in formulating, promoting, and executing the plans for this book; and James Bell and John Drayton have provided moral and editorial support. Appreciation and gratitude are expressed to all.

Theoretical Foundations

The Arts
and the Spirit
of the Lord*

Elder Boyd K. Packer

I am particularly appreciative of the music we've just heard, and quote from section 25 of the Doctrine and Covenants: "For my soul delighteth in the song of the heart: yea, the song of the righteous is a prayer unto me, and it shall be answered with a blessing upon their heads" (D&C 25:12).

I very anxiously lay claim to those blessings from these righteous young men and women who have sung so beautifully this sacred hymn of Zion. My gratitude to them will, I'm sure, be more obvious when I move into the message that I have chosen to speak upon tonight.

I want to respond to a question that I face with some frequency. It has many variations, but the theme is this: Why do we not have more inspired and inspiring music in the Church? Or why do we have so few great paintings or sculptures depicting the Restoration? Why is it when we need a new painting for a bureau of information, or perhaps for a temple, frequently nonmember painters receive the commission? The same questions have an application to poetry, to drama, to dance, to creative writing, to all the fine arts.

Now, I'm sure there are those who will say, "Why does he presume to talk about that? He is uninformed. He is just out of his province." It may comfort them to know that I know that.

*Reprinted from *1976 Devotional Speeches of the Year* (Provo: Brigham Young University Press, 1977), pp. 265–82.

My credentials to speak do not come from being a musician, for I'm not. I am not a composer, nor a conductor, and certainly I am not a vocalist. I cannot, for example, play the piano. I would be very unwilling to do so. However, should I be pressed to it, I could, without much difficulty, prove my point. I am not adequate as an artist, nor as a sculptor, a poet, or a writer.

But then I do not intend to train you in any of those fields. My credentials, if I have any (some of them should be obvious), relate to spiritual things.

I hope for sufficient inspiration to comment on how the Spirit of the Lord influences or is influenced by the art forms that I have mentioned. Since I have been interested in these matters, I have, over the years, listened very carefully when they have been discussed by the Brethren. I have studied expressions of my Brethren and of those who have led us in times past in order to determine how those questions should be answered.

The reason we have not yet produced a greater heritage in art and literature and music and drama is not, I am very certain, because we have not had talented people. For over the years we have had not only good ones but great ones. Some have reached great heights in their chosen fields. But few have captured the spirit of the gospel of Jesus Christ and the restoration of it in music, in art, in literature. They have not, therefore, even though they were gifted, made a lasting contribution to the onrolling of the Church and kingdom of God in the dispensation of the fulness of times. They have therefore missed doing what they might have done, and they have missed being what they might have become. I am reminded of the statement, "There are many who struggle and climb and finally reach the top of the ladder, only to find that it is leaning against the wrong wall."

If you are willing to listen, I would like to express some concerns I have had over these matters and describe to you some disappointments I have heard expressed among the leaders of the Church.

Because I intend to be quite direct in my comments, I am a bit concerned. For I know when we touch this subject we talk of people who are very gifted. And people who are very gifted, it would seem, tend to be temperamental.

We were discussing some time ago the music and musicians of the Church, when one of the Twelve pointed out that it may be difficult to get instruction across because some of our musicians, among others, have a tendency to be temperamental. "Yes," observed one of the senior members of our Quorum, "More temper than mental." That, I suppose, describes all of us at one time or another.

Before I continue, I want it clearly understood that we have in the Church tens of thousands of gifted people who not only have talent, but who are generous with it. Our gifted people are greatly needed in the Church.

The work of the Lord has been moved by the members in the wards and stakes and branches who have been blessed with special gifts and who use them unselfishly. Because of what they do, we are able to feel and learn very quickly through music, through art, through poetry some spiritual things that we would otherwise learn very slowly. All of us are indebted to them for their generous service. I am humbly grateful to those who render such service in the Church. But then it is only right that they should contribute.

You who have such talents might well ask, "Whence comes this gift?" And gift it is. You may have cultivated it and developed it, but it was given to you. Most of us do not have it. You were not more deserving than we, but you are a good deal more responsible. If you use your gift properly, opportunities for service are opened that will be beneficial eternally for you and for others.

Has it ever occurred to you that you may leave this life without it? If the gift is yours because of the shape of your vocal cords, or the strength of your lungs, or because of the coordination of your hands, or because your eye registers form and color, you may leave the gift behind. You may have to be content with what you have become because you possessed it while you were here. It has not been revealed just how this would be. I rather suspect that those gifts which we use properly will stay with us beyond the veil. And I repeat, you who are gifted may not be more deserving, but you are much more responsible than the rest of us.

Elder Orson F. Whitney said:

> We shall yet have Miltons and Shakespeares of our own. God's ammunition is not exhausted. His highest spirits are held in reserve for the latter times. In God's name and by His help we will build up a literature whose tops will touch the heaven, though its foundation may now be low on the earth.[1]

Since that statement was made in 1888, those foundations have been raised up very slowly. The greatest poems are not yet written, nor the paintings finished. The greatest hymns and anthems of the Restoration are yet to be composed. The sublimest renditions of them are yet to be conducted. We move forward much slower than need be, and I would like to underline some things that stand in our way.

You will quickly notice that I refer frequently to music. There is a reason for that. We use it more often. But the point that I shall make about the musician applies to all the arts: painting, poetry, drama, dance, and others.

For some reason it takes a constant vigilance on the part of priesthood leaders—both general and local—to ensure that music presented in our worship and devotional services is music appropriate for worship and devotional services. I have heard presidents of the Church declare after a general conference or after a temple dedication words to this effect (and I am quoting verbatim from one such experience):

> I suppose we did not give enough attention to the music. It seems that our musicians must take such liberties. Something spiritual was lost from our meetings because the music was not what it should have been. Next time we must remember to give them more careful instructions.

Why is it that the President of the Church, or the president of the stake, or the bishop of the ward must be so attentive in arranging music for worship services and conference meetings? Why should the anxiety persist that, if the musicians are left to do what they want to do, the result will not invite the Spirit of the Lord?

I have in the past made not altogether successful attempts to set a mood of devotion on a very sacred subject, having been invited to the pulpit immediately after a choral number that was well performed but did nothing to inspire the spirit of devotion; or after a brass ensemble has rendered music that has nothing to do with spiritual inspiration.

The selections, which for other purposes might have been admirable, even impressive, failed in their inspiration simply because they were not appropriate. For some other gathering, some other time, some other place, yes—but they did not do what the hymns of the Restoration could have done. How sad when a gifted person has no real sense of propriety.

Let me illustrate this matter of propriety. Suppose you sponsor a pep rally in the stadium with the purpose of exciting the student body to a high point of enthusiasm. Suppose you invite someone to present a musical number with the expectation that the music would contribute to your purpose. Imagine him playing a sonata on an organ in subdued tones that lull everyone into a contemplative and reflective mood. However well composed the music, or however well performed, it would not be appropriate for the occasion.

This example, of course, is obvious. It makes me wonder, therefore, why we must be constantly alert to have appropriate music in our sacrament meetings, conference sessions, and other worship services. Music and art and dance and literature can be very appropriate in one place and in one setting and for one purpose and be very wrong in another. That can be true of instruments as well.

We have, in our instruction to the musicians of the Church, this suggestion:

> Organs and pianos are the standard musical instruments used in sacrament meetings. Other instruments, such as orchestral strings, may be used when appropriate, but the music presented must be in keeping with the reverence and spirituality of the meeting. Brass and percussion instruments generally are not appropriate.[2]

We are under resistance from some highly trained musicians who insist that they can get as much inspiration from brass instruments or a guitar solo as from a choir. I believe that an organ perhaps could be played at a pep rally in a way to incite great enthusiasm. And I think a brass section could play a hymn in such a way as to be reverent and fitting in a worship service. But that would have to be an exception. We cannot convey a sacred message in an art form that is not appropriate and have anything spiritual happen. But there is a constant attempt to do it.

Several years ago one of the organizations of the Church produced a filmstrip. The subject matter was very serious and the script was well written. The producer provided a story board, which is a series of loose, almost scribbled sketches, sometimes with a little color brushed across them, to roughly illustrate each frame of the filmstrip. Very little work is invested in a story board. It is merely to give an idea and is always subject to revision.

Some members of the committee were amused by the story board itself. It had a loose, comical air about it. They decided to photograph the illustrations on the story board and use them in the filmstrip. They thought the illustrations would be quite amusing and entertaining.

When the filmstrip was reviewed by four members of the Council of the Twelve, it was rejected. It had to be made over again. Why? Because the art form used simply was not appropriate to the message. You just don't teach sacred, serious subjects with careless, scribbled illustrations.

Now, again to music. There have been a number of efforts to take sacred gospel themes and tie them to modern music in the hope of attracting our young people to the message. Few events in all of human history surpass the spiritual majesty of the First Vision. We would be ill-advised to describe that event, the visit of Elohim and Jehovah, in company with rock music, even soft rock music, or to take equally sacred themes and set them to a modern beat. I do not know how that can be done and result in increased spirituality. I think it cannot be done.

When highly trained artists insist, as they occasionally do, that they receive spiritual experience in tying a sacred gospel theme to an inappropriate art form, I must conclude that they do not know, not really, the difference between when the Spirit of the Lord is present and when it is not.

Very frequently when our musicians, particularly the more highly trained among them, are left to do what they want to do, they perform in such a way as to call attention to themselves and their ability. They do this rather than give prayerful attention to what will inspire. I do not mean "inspire" as the music or art of the world can inspire. I mean *inspire!*

They are not content to use the hymns and anthems of the Restoration, for such a presentation, they feel, will not demonstrate their full capacities. When pressed to do so, they may grudgingly put a hymn on the program. But it is obvious that their heart isn't in it, for the numbers they select themselves seem to say, "Now let us show you what we really can do."

We instruct stake presidents, "Preference should be given to the singing of well-known hymns" at stake conferences.[3]

I know there are those who think that our Church music is limited. Some with professional abilities evidently soon get very tired of it. They want to stray from it and reach out into the world. They present the argument that many of the hymns in our hymnbook were not written for the Church or by members of the Church. I know that already. And some of them are not really as compelling as they might be. Their messages are not as specific as we could have if we produced our own. But by association they have taken on a meaning that reminds members of the Church, whenever they hear them, of the restoration of the gospel, of the Lord, and of His ministry.

Sometimes, to ensure that music will be appropriate, one of the hymns or anthems of the Restoration is specifically requested. "Oh, but they sang that last conference," our conductors will say. Indeed we did, and we preached the same gospel last conference also. The preaching of it over and over again gives it a familiar and a warm feeling. We build it into our lives.

As speakers we are not trying to impress the world with how talented we are as preachers. We are simply trying to get across, by repetition, if that's the only way, the sacred message that has been entrusted to us.

Those of us who lead the Church are not constantly seeking new doctrine to introduce. We simply teach over and over again that which was in the beginning. It is with great difficulty that we try to pass on to the next generation, in some form of purity, that which was given to us. We will lose it if we are not wise.

The musician may say, "Do you really want us to take those few familiar hymns and present them over and over again with no introduction of anything new?" No, that is not what I would want, but it is close.

What I would desire would be to have the hymns of the Restoration *characteristic* of our worship services, with others added if they are appropriate. There are a great many things from elsewhere that are very appropriate. Many numbers can be used in our worship services with complete propriety.

Our hymns speak the truth as far as they go. They could speak more of it if we had more of them, specifically teaching the principles of the restored gospel of Jesus Christ.

If I had my way there would be many new hymns with lyrics near scriptural in their power, bonded to music that would inspire people to worship. Think how much we could be helped by another inspired anthem or hymn of the Restoration. Think how we could be helped by an inspired painting on a scriptural theme or depicting our heritage. How much we could be aided by a graceful and modest dance, by a persuasive narrative, or poem, or drama. We could have the Spirit of the Lord more frequently and in almost unlimited intensity if we would.

For the most part, we do without because the conductor wants to win the acclaim of the world. He does not play to the Lord, but to other musicians. The composer and the arranger want to please the world. The painter wants to be in style. And so our resources of art and music grow ever so gradually. And we find that there have marched through this grand parade of mortality men and women who were sublimely gifted, but who spent all, or most, in the world and for the world. And I repeat that they may well one day come to learn that "many men struggle to reach the top of the ladder, only to find that it is leaning against the wrong wall."

It is a mistake to assume that one can follow the ways of the world and then somehow, in a moment of intruded inspiration, compose a great anthem of the Restoration, or in a moment of singular inspiration paint the great painting. When it is done, it will be done by one who has yearned and tried and longed fervently to do it, not by one who has condescended to do it. It will take quite as much preparation and work as would any masterpiece, and a different kind of inspiration.

There is a test you might apply if you are among the gifted. Ask yourself this question: "When I am free to do what I really want to do, what will it be?"

If you find that you are ashamed of our humble heritage in the arts, that ought to be something of a signal to you. Often artists are not free to create what they most desire because the market demands other things of them. But what about when you are free? Do you have a desire to produce what the Church needs? Or do you desire to convince the Church that it needs to change style so the world will feel comfortable with it? Although our artistic heritage as yet is relatively small, we are losing some of what we have—through neglect!

At the recent rededication of the St. George Temple each session was closed, as is traditional in a temple dedication, with the presentation of the "Hosanna Anthem." The audience, on the signal from the conductor, joins with the choir on that part of the anthem known widely through the Church as "The Spirit of God Like a Fire Is Burning." I sat through those sessions and carefully observed, with great sorrow, that fully 80 percent of those in the audience did not know the words.

We can lose our heritage. We have lost part of it. Let me cite an example in the field of poetry.

William Ernest Henley wrote "Invictus," a proud, almost defiant expression that concludes:

> I am the master of my fate,
> I am the captain of my soul.

Some years ago an answer to "Invictus" was given. Let me quote it to you:

> Art thou in truth?
> Then what of Him who bought thee with His blood?
> Who plunged into devouring seas
> And snatched thee from the flood,
>
> Who bore for all our fallen race
> What none but Him could bear—
> That God who died that man might live
> And endless glory share.
>
> Of what avail thy vaunted strength
> Apart from His vast might?
> Pray that His light may pierce the gloom
> That thou mayest see aright.
>
> Men are as bubbles on the wave,
> As leaves upon the tree,
> Thou, captain of thy soul! Forsooth,
> Who gave that place to thee?
>
> Free will is thine—free agency,
> To wield for right or wrong;
> But thou must answer unto Him
> To whom all souls belong.
>
> Bend to the dust that "head unbowed,"
> Small part of life's great whole,
> And see in Him and Him alone,
> The captain of thy soul.[4]

And who wrote that? Orson F..Whitney of the Council of the Twelve Apostles, a gifted and inspired poet whose work is virtually unknown in the Church.

Let me quote another of his poems:

> There's a mountain named Stern Justice,
> Tall and towering, gloomy, grand,
> Frowning o'er a vale called Mercy,
> Loveliest in all the land.
>
> Great and mighty is the mountain,
> But its snowy crags are cold,
> And in vain the sunlight lingers
> On the summit proud and bold.
>
> There is warmth within the valley,
> And I love to wander there,
> 'Mid the fountains and the flowers,
> Breathing fragrance on the air.
>
> Much I love the solemn mountain,
> It doth meet my somber mood,
> When, amid the muttering thunders,
> O'er my soul the storm-clouds brood.
>
> But when tears, like rain, have fallen
> From the fountain of my woe,
> And my soul has lost its fierceness,
> Straight unto the vale I go;
>
> Where the landscape, gently smiling,
> O'er my heart pours healing balm,
> And, as oil on troubled waters,
> Brings from out its storm a calm.
>
> Yes, I love both vale and mountain,
> Ne'er from either would I part;
> Each unto my life is needful,
> Both are dear unto my heart.
>
> For the smiling vale doth soften
> All the rugged steep makes sad,
> And from icy rocks meander
> Rills that make the valley glad.[5]

Both of these poems are new to most of you. Why would that be? I think it more than a pity that work such as this remains unknown to most students and faculty—even to some of the faculty in the field of literature. It is sad when members of the faculty here would discard them in favor of assigning their students to read degenerate compositions that issue from the minds of perverted and wicked men.

There is the temptation for college teachers, in the Church and outside of it, to exercise their authority to give assignments and thereby introduce their students to degradation under the argument that it is part of our culture. Teachers in the field of literature are particularly vulnerable.

I use the word *warning*. Such will not go unnoticed in the eternal scheme of things. Those who convey a degraded heritage to the next generation will reap disappointment by and by.

Teachers would do well to learn the difference between studying some things, as compared to studying *about* them. There is a great difference.

There is much to be said for a great effort to rediscover the humble and inspired contributions of gifted Saints of the past and thereby inspire the gifted in our day to produce works that will inspire those who come after us.

It is sad but true that, almost as a rule, our most gifted members are drawn to the world. They who are most capable of preserving our cultural heritage and extending it, because of the enticements of the world, seek rather to replace it. That is so easy to do because for the most part they do not have that intent. They think that what they do is to improve it. Unfortunately many of them will live to learn that indeed, "Many men struggle to climb to reach the top of the ladder, only to find that it is leaning against the wrong wall."

I mentioned earlier that the greatest hymns and anthems have not been composed, nor have the greatest illustrations been set down, nor the poems written, nor the paintings finished. When they are produced, who will produce them? Will it be the most talented and the most highly trained among us? I rather think it will not. They will be produced by those who are the most inspired among us. Inspiration can come to those whose talents are barely adequate, and their contribution will be felt for generations; and the Church and kingdom of God will move forward just a little more easily because they have been here.

Some of our most gifted people struggle to produce a work of art, hoping that it will be described by the world as a masterpiece! monumental! epic! when in truth the simple, compelling theme of "I Am a Child of God" has moved and will move more souls to salvation than would such a work were they to succeed.

Some years ago I was chairman of a committee of seminary men responsible for producing a filmstrip on Church history. One of the group, Trevor Christensen, remembered that down in Sanpete County was a large canvas roll of paintings. They had been painted by one of his progenitors, C. C. A. Christensen, who traveled through the settlements giving a lecture on Church history as each painting was unrolled and displayed by lamplight. The roll of paintings had been stored away for generations. We sent a truck for them, and I shall not forget the day we unrolled it.

Brother Christensen was not masterful in his painting, but our heritage was there. Some said it was not great art, but what it lacked in technique was more than compensated for in feeling. His work has been shown more widely and published more broadly and received more attention than that of a thousand and one others who missed that point.

I do not think Brother Christensen was a great painter, some would say not even a good one. But I do think his paintings are masterful. Why? Because the simple, reverent feeling he had for his spiritual heritage is captured in them. I do not think it strange that the world would honor a man who could not paint very well.

The ideal, of course, is for one with a gift to train and develop it to the highest possibility, including a sense of spiritual propriety. No artist in the Church who desires unselfishly to extend our heritage need sacrifice his career or an avocation, nor need he neglect his gift as only a hobby. He can meet the world and "best" it, and not be the loser. In the end, what appears to be such sacrifice will have been but a test.

Abraham did not have to kill Isaac, you know. He had to be willing to. Once that was known, that he would sacrifice his only begotten, he was known to be godlike and the blessings. poured out upon him.

A few years ago Sister Packer and I were in Washington, D.C., to represent the Church at an awards banquet held in the reception hall of the Department of State. The elegant and stately surroundings, with a priceless collection of antiques and memorabilia, were impressive. Here, for instance, hangs the painting of

George Washington by Gilbert Stuart. Both the occasion and the setting were ideal to make reference to the spiritual heritage of our country. And what was the program? A large brass section from one of the service bands played at great length, and with deafening volume, music from *Jesus Christ, Superstar.*

I sat next to a lovely, dignified woman, the wife of an officer of the government. When the crescendo weakened for a moment, I was able to ask, by raising my voice a bit, if she was able to hear them all right. Her obvious amusement at the question soon changed to serious disappointment, as she asked in return, "What would Jesus think?"

That is well worth keeping in our minds if we have the talent to compose music or poetry, to illustrate or paint, or sculpt or act, or sing or play or conduct.

What do I think He would think? I think He would rejoice at the playing of militant martial music as men marched to defend a righteous cause. I think that He would think there are times when illustrations should be vigorous, with bold and exciting colors. I think He would chuckle with approval when at times of recreation the music is comical or melodramatic or exciting. Or at times when a carnival air is in order that decorations be bright and flashy, even garish.

I think at times of entertainment He would think it quite in order for poetry that would make one laugh or cry—perhaps both at once. I think that He would think it would be in righteous order on many occasions to perform with great dignity symphonies and operas and ballets. I think that He would think that soloists should develop an extensive repertoire, each number to be performed at a time and in a place that is appropriate.

I would think that He would think there is a place for art work of every kind—from the scribbled cartoon to the masterpiece in the hand-carved, gold-leaf frame.

But I am sure He would be offended at immodesty and irreverence in music, in art, in poetry, in writing, in sculpture, in dance, or in drama. I know what He would think about music or art or literature or poetry that is purely secular being introduced into our worship services. And how do I know that? Because He has told His servants that. In what ways has He told them? He has told them by either withholding, or on occasions withdrawing, His Spirit when it is done.

I mentioned earlier that I have sometimes struggled without much success to teach sacred things when preceded by music that is secular or uninspired. Let me mention the other side of it.

I have been in places where I felt insecure and unprepared. I have yearned inwardly in great agony for some power to pave the way or loosen my tongue, that an opportunity would not be lost because of my weakness and inadequacy. On more than a few occasions my prayers have been answered by the power of inspired music. I have been lifted above myself and beyond myself when the Spirit of the Lord has poured in upon the meeting, drawn there by beautiful, appropriate music. I stand indebted to the gifted among us who have that unusual sense of spiritual propriety.

Go to, then, you who are gifted; cultivate your gift. Develop it in any of the arts and in every worthy example of them. If you have the ability and the desire, seek a career or employ your talent as an avocation or cultivate it as a hobby. But in all ways bless others with it. Set a standard of excellence. Employ it in the secular sense to every worthy advantage, but never use it profanely. Never express your gift unworthily. Increase our spiritual heritage in music, in art, in literature, in dance, in drama.

When we have done it our activities will be a standard to the world. And our worship and devotion will remain as unique from the world as the Church is different from the world. Let the use of your gift be an expression of your devotion to Him who has given it to you. We who do not share in it will set a high standard of expectation: "For of him unto whom much is given much is required" (D&C 82:3).

Now, in conclusion, may I remind you what I said at the beginning. My credential to speak does not come from personal mastery of the arts. I repeat my confession. I am not gifted as a musician or as a poet, nor adequate as an artist, nor accomplished in the field of dance, or writing, or drama. I speak on this subject because I have a calling, one which not only permits, but even requires, that we stay close to Him and to His Spirit.

If we know nothing of the arts, we know something of the Spirit. We know that it can be drawn upon meagerly or almost to the consuming of an individual.

In 1832 the Prophet Joseph Smith received a revelation which now stands as section 88 of the Doctrine and Covenants and was designated by the Prophet as "The Olive Leaf." I quote a few verses:

Draw near unto me and I will draw near unto you; seek
me diligently and ye shall find me; ask, and ye shall receive;
knock, and it shall be opened unto you.

Whatsoever ye ask the Father in my name it shall be
given unto you, that is expedient for you;

And if ye ask anything that is not expedient for you, it
shall turn unto your condemnation.

Behold, that which you hear is as the voice of one
crying in the wilderness—in the wilderness, because you
cannot see him—my voice, because my voice is Spirit; my
Spirit is truth; truth abideth and hath no end; and if it be in
you it shall abound.

And if your eye be single to my glory, your whole
bodies shall be filled with light, and there shall be no
darkness in you; and that body which is filled with light
comprehendeth all things.

Therefore, sanctify yourselves that your minds become
single to God, and the days will come that you shall see
him; for he will unveil his face unto you, and it shall be in
his own time, and in his own way, and according to his own
will. [D&C 88:63–68]

The Spirit of the Lord can be present on His terms only. God
grant that we may learn, each of us, particularly those who are
gifted, how to extend that invitation.

He lives. Of Him I bear witness. Jesus is the Christ, the Son
of God, the Only Begotten of the Father. Spencer W. Kimball is
a prophet of God. We have on our shoulders in this generation
the Church and kingdom of God to bear away. God grant that
those among us who are the most gifted will devote themselves in
order that our task may be easier, I pray in the name of Jesus
Christ. Amen.

*Because of the interest generated when this address was given at a
Twelve-Stake Fireside on 1 February 1976 at Brigham Young University,
Monday Magazine, a campus weekly, sent writer Bruce D. Porter to
Salt Lake City to interview Elder Packer about fine arts in the Church.*

Arts in the Gospel: An Interview*

Monday Magazine: In your fireside address you spoke about
the importance of choosing appropriate musical works for

*Reprinted from *Daily Universe, Monday Magazine,* 17 February 1976, p. 20.

performance in our worship services. "The hymns of the Restoration" were what you mentioned most often. What other works are appropriate?

Elder Packer: I said in my address that our hymns should be "characteristic" of the music we choose from our worship service. That doesn't mean hymns must be the only thing played, but they should predominate, and other pieces chosen should be of a similar worshipful and reverent spirit.... We can benefit from these works, but we have to choose with care. There's a place for art of every kind—but that place is not necessarily in our church meetings.

Monday Magazine: Do you believe that the secular art of the world has something to offer us, if not introduced into our worship services?

Elder Packer: Yes, definitely. I have enjoyed and been uplifted by a variety of symphonies, operas, and ballets many times. There is no question that the musical tradition of the world has much to give us—in the proper time and place. I recall, for example, attending an opera in London which was very inspiring to me.

Monday Magazine: In what sense can a secular work of art be inspiring?

Elder Packer: I use the word *inspire* deliberately, because it seems to be the best word. The secular music and art of the world can inspire us in a very good and valuable way—but it is not the inspiration of the Holy Spirit. That is something very different, and it's important not to confuse the two.

There are a few paintings in the museums of the world which I consider to be of great and "inspiring" beauty. There are a couple of paintings in Paris I try to see whenever I go there—if there's time. I consider it worth the investment just to see them. But the inspiration of such a painting is not the same as the inspiration that comes through the direct presence of the Lord's spirit. It is not the same inspiration we seek to feel in our worship services.

Monday Magazine: In your fireside address you discussed the contribution of the pioneer painter C. C. A. Christensen. You mentioned that his technique was not as polished as some but that "what it lacked in technique was more than compensated for in feeling." Would you make a distinction, then, between technique and content in the fine arts?

Elder Packer: Yes I would. I think the content is where our Latter-day Saint artists must put their first emphasis, but it would be best if we could get superior technique combined with it. Once again, I think the answer is in my fireside address. Only a combination of highly trained talent and divine inspiration could produce the truly great masterpiece: "When it is done, it will be done by one who has longed and yearned and prayed fervently to do it.... It will take quite as much preparation and work and time as any masterpiece and ... a different kind of inspiration."

Monday Magazine: Are there any artists in the Church moving in this direction?

Elder Packer: Oh, yes, there are many. I think immediately of Merrill Bradshaw's excellent oratorio, *The Restoration,* and there are others. But we could be having so much more if our talented and gifted Saints were only willing to give more to the Church.

Monday Magazine: Brother Packer, there has apparently been some confusion among students of literature at BYU as to what exactly your viewpoint on literature is. You warned teachers against assigning students to read degraded works. What would you consider "degraded"?

Elder Packer: Anything that doesn't uplift. There is certainly much among the great literature of the world which is very uplifting, and I hope that no student uses my talk as an excuse not to study literature in depth. But there are many works that have been written in our century—and some in past centuries—which are evil and perverted and should not be assigned to students to read.

Monday Magazine: Is it possible for literature to deal with themes of sin or destitution in a way that is not degraded, that could be considered moral and worthy of reading?

Elder Packer: Yes, that is possible. The way in which certain things are presented becomes very important in judging. Now, I consider Shakespeare a great writer. I've always enjoyed him; I've read most of his works. But I certainly wouldn't quote certain lines from his plays in sacrament meeting.

Unfortunately, nowadays our writers not only want to deal with themes of human weakness, they insist on doing it in living color—and such literature (or film or art) is corrupting and evil. A generation ago if a dramatist wanted to portray a girl of the streets, it was done by the way her earrings dangled and the way she chewed gum. The impression that she was a cheap woman could be conveyed without her being dressed suggestively. But now artists and writers overdo it. They give the audience no credit for intelligence.

Monday Magazine: But if done tastefully, there might be some value in a story about immorality or a broken family?

Elder Packer: Yes. But I am saddened that that seems to be the only kind of theme so many writers deal with. They seem to think nothing else has dramatic value. As a result the only kind of family we ever see in literature and on the stage is the broken, problem family. That isn't realistic. I wish some writer would learn to portray the joy of a solid, righteous family in an artistic, uplifting way.

Monday Magazine: What do you hope will be the general response to your fireside address?

Elder Packer (laughing): Well, I guess it wouldn't have accomplished anything if it didn't disturb a few people. I've never given a major address that hasn't received a number of very critical responses. But it is one of the duties of my calling to exhort the Saints, to set the Church in order, and I can't ignore that duty. Sometimes, I know, misunderstandings take place simply because it is impossible to cover every ramification of a theme in a talk. It's like traveling through a canyon. There are many side roads I could have taken that would have clarified certain points more finely, but time allowed me to take only a simple, direct route.

When I delivered that address I was very aware that it would be listened to on radio and television, that it would be printed and go to many parts of the nation and world. Some of my remarks were directed to that larger audience—by no means only to BYU. In fact, I can say I have a very great faith generally in the judgment and quality of the faculty and students of BYU. Many of my warnings were directed less toward them than toward Latter-day Saint artists and professionals not at BYU who will read my talk. I hope my talk will be read and pondered particularly by those very gifted and talented Saints who may be climbing the wrong ladder. I know they have a very important and great contribution to make to the Church, if only they would.

I know of only one source I can go to in order to decide what to speak about on a given occasion. Sometimes I fidget around and delay and wait before going to that source—but I know it's the only one. I went to Him to determine the subject of my fireside address, and I sought His help in preparing it. I'm sure you know what I'm talking about.

Notes

1. "Home Literature," in *A Believing People,* ed. Richard H. Cracroft and Neal E. Lambert (Provo, Utah: Brigham Young University Press, 1974), p. 206.

2. *General Handbook of Instructions* (Salt Lake City: The Church of Jesus Christ of Latter-day Saints, 1976), p. 23.

3. 1976 Stake Conference Schedules.

4. "The Soul's Captain," from *Two Poems* (n.p., n.d.).

5. "The Mountain and the Vale," *Poetical Writings of Orson F. Whitney* (Salt Lake City: Juvenile Instructor Office, 1889), p. 183.

Insights from the Outside: Thoughts for the Mormon Writer*

Candadai Seshachari

It seems that in most discussions of Mormon letters, two literary concerns inevitably emerge. Not so surprisingly, at the bottom of both these issues is the question of the relationship between literature and dogma. Since dogma and Church fiat control much of what the faithful write, can Mormon letters, it is asked, break through the mold of teleological and eschatological givens to become a literature of significance outside its own confines?

The other concern questions whether Mormon literature is, because of its "Mormonness," too exclusive in its subject matter and too facile in its world view to be meaningful to a non-Mormon audience. Can a Mormon literary work be intellectually, emotionally, and aesthetically "accessible" to readers who do not relate to Mormonism? Even editors Richard Cracroft and Neal Lambert in their anthology, *A Believing People: Literature of the Latter-day Saints,* seem to have these concerns in mind when they say that "Mormons characteristically continue to see the world through a paradisiacal glass, brightly," and that essentially "Mormon writing is outside the mainstream of modern literary fashion."[1]

In the first of these arguments, I fail to see how one could set aside—even sublimate—one's past, one's culture, in a sense, one's being, and compose a literary work that's the life blood of one's

*Reprinted, by permission, from *Dialogue: A Journal of Mormon Thought* 11, no. 2 (1978): 90–92.

spirit, as Milton would have said. Indeed, why should one disregard one's teleological or religious predilections? Would Milton be more Milton if he disregarded his strong, sometimes even perverse, theological convictions? Or is his theology the very bedrock of his literary genius? More fundamentally, could a writer neglect the very stuff of his being and yet somehow remain himself and whole? Perhaps this question of the relationship between dogma and literature was best answered by novelist V. S. Prichett. In a letter to fellow novelist Graham Greene, he appropriately argued:

> You point to the dangers of the religious groups who wish to impose a certain spiritual life; but there are the political groups too, the totalitarian, the socialist, the liberal, and also the huge jelly fish composed of deadly, transparent people who believe they belong to no group at all, which desire to impose upon the writer.[2]

Of course this imposition by a group is not just inevitable; it is the very condition of human existence. As inevitably, the Mormon writer brings his unique experience to probe and define the complexities of the human condition. It is through this singular experience that he asserts his individuality, indeed his humanity. This experience defines his being. If one takes away from him the memory of the martyrdom of Joseph Smith, the tragedy and the heroism of the exodus of his ancestors, as well as the everyday details that made Zion happen, it is like blotting out the story of Christ from a Christian's consciousness, or like rooting out the fact of slavery from the racial memory of the American black. Bereft of his "Mormonness," which saturates all levels of his conscious and unconscious mind, the Mormon writer is naught, unfit both as subject matter and creator of literary works. What Carl Becker said of the historian is even more apropos of the writer: "The historian and his concepts are part of the very process he would interpret.... He is not outside history as the chemist is outside chemistry."[3] The writer's subjectivity is what quickens his art.

For the Mormon writer, the creative center of this subjectivity lies not so much in what he shares with the rest of mankind but in that unique Mormon experience which he shares with fellow Mormons. He does not however forsake the literary symbols and metaphors to which he is generally heir; to these he adds other symbols and metaphors from his own Mormon experience. To the problems of human existence he brings an affirmation of faith and vision which had lighted the path of his own ancestors.

If to every writer's credo there is a source of life-giving inspiration which sustains his art, then to the Mormon writer the wellsprings of his art lie in his dogma. All of this in no sense makes Mormon literature any more inaccessible to the readers than is John Bunyan's *Pilgrim's Progress* or Jonathan Edwards's "Sinners in the Hands of an Angry God" to the readers of our generation or, for that matter, Raja Rao's *Kanthapura* is to non-Indian readers or Yasunari Kawabata's *Snow Country* is to readers who have not enjoyed the fleshly companionship of a geisha. The subject matter of all literature, in any age or clime, deals both with the universe in which we live and with the predicament and exaltation of human existence. Whether the characters have an unpronounceable Russian or an incomprehensible East Indian name, or whether the flora and fauna of the setting have anything in common with the native American genus or species is not of much consequence to a reader's imaginative involvement with a work of art. Ultimately all literature becomes vital at the imaginative level which, in turn, is essentially vicarious, but no less real.

Thus the Mormon writer, like any other artist, imparts to his works a sense of his own values or vision. The vision sometimes may be too simplistic or too complex, too dismal or too optimistic, but in no way can the writer separate the substance of his writing from the substance of his being, whether he be a Mormon or Hindu, a raving liberal or diehard radical. That is as it should be, for the reader can experience every kind of emotion and can recognize every kind of idea. But whether he will equally enjoy all works of art alike or subscribe to all ideas is a different argument altogether.

It is a truism that even though literary works give aesthetic pleasure and engender feelings of empathy, they do not necessarily create an identity of views in the readers. For instance, who would not be moved by the way Alma, the old man in Herbert Harker's recent novel *Turn Again Home,* meets his end, which he imploringly seeks, at the hands of Hickory Jack. Alma had wanted to see his own blood flow as an act of atonement for his part in the Mountain Meadows massacre. The pain of living had been too much for him, but the irony of ironies was that Hickory Jack, in the act of helping Alma expiate his own sin, had shot Alma point-blank. "I forgot he wanted to see the blood," Hickory Jack intoned in recollecting the incident.[4] An utter sense of waste pervades the ending of the novel. To revert to the question: How crucial is it to one's aesthetic enjoyment of the novel to be aware of the doctrine of blood atonement which some saints subscribed to in the agonizing days of the early persecution of Mormons?

In the foregoing discussion I have not dealt with the general quality of Mormon literature nor the achievements of its significant writers. The literary merit of a work is independent of whether it falls within the realm of Mormon literature or some other literary classification. A work must be able to stand scrutiny in terms of well-recognized canons of criticism. A Mormon writer's inherent right to his subject matter is no passport for him to be judged differently—or indifferently.

At this point, I can do no better than narrate an incident which Booker T. Washington mentions in his famous Atlanta Exposition Address. A ship which had lost its bearings at sea, on sighting a friendly vessel, signaled: "Water, water; we die of thirst!" And the other ship replied, "Cast down your bucket where you are." A second, third, and fourth plea for water was similarly answered. The captain of the distressed vessel, finally heeding the injunction, let down his bucket to come up with fresh thirst-quenching water from the Amazon.⁵ Likewise, the Mormon writer should cast down his bucket into the life-giving waters of his own culture and into the stream of his own inner self. He can do no less; to do otherwise would be to betray himself and his craft.

Notes

1. Richard Cracroft and Neal Lambert, "Introduction," *A Believing People: Literature of the Latter-Day Saints* (Provo, Utah: Brigham Young University Press, 1974), p. 5.

2. V. S. Prichett, *Why Do I Write* (London: Percival Marshall, 1948), p. 34.

3. Carl Becker, *Detachment and the Writing of History: Essays and Letters of Carl Becker* (Ithaca, N.Y.: Cornell University Press, 1958), p. 21.

4. Herbert Harker, *Turn Again Home* (New York: Random House, 1977), p. 244.

5. Booker T. Washington, "Atlanta Exposition Address," *The Rhetoric of Black Americans,* ed. James Golden and Richard Rieke (Columbus, Ohio: Charles Merrill Publishing Co., 1971), p. 113.

Religion Versus Art:
Can the Ancient Conflict
be Resolved?

Wayne C. Booth

When I was a boy in American Fork, I was "taught" that art is a luxury or a decoration, sometimes dangerous, often wasteful, and always secondary to the serious pursuits of life. Nobody taught me all this in so many words. Nobody said directly that the serious business of life had nothing to do with art, but that's what was taught by the way our lives were run.

The teaching varied, of course, as it pertained to different arts. Music was a good thing to have around, and we were told wonderful stories about how it had served our pioneer grandparents in time of hardship. Music lessons were, I'm grateful to say, taken for granted for all in the family, somehow squeezed out of our always borderline budget. But it would have troubled everyone, I think, if anyone in the family had decided to "become a musician"—as indeed it did trouble everyone when one uncle joined a dance band instead of going to college. Literature was less important than music, and more dangerous. And visual art was so far down the scale that it was not even mentioned. Two or three of our elementary teachers did require us to "draw," for reasons I never understood, but nobody I knew had ever voluntarily painted or sculpted anything.

Though my parents and grandparents had books in the house, including of course Shakespeare and Wordsworth, some Dickens, and even some of the less offensive works of Mark Twain, I cannot remember seeing anyone sit down to read a book for the sake of reading it—reading it for sheer pleasure, as we say, though the word has always been misleading as a description of our reasons for pursuing art works for the joys of the pursuit itself. What's more, I can remember hundreds of times when I was accused of wasting my time reading in some corner (somehow always in a bad light: "You'll ruin your eyes!"), instead of—well, instead of doing something serious: working, doing homework (which never had anything to do with art), preparing my two-and-one-half-minute talks. One grandfather even had a theory that it was wicked to read any "stories" except the Bible.

It is easy to explain, in historical and sociological terms, why the arts were played down in our lives in the twenties. There were still among us many who had been born and raised in conditions of bare survival, and art is not essential for bare survival. Art is a product of surplus, a luxury, depending for its production and appreciation on at least some slight release from the daily struggle for food and shelter. And it is natural that the first arts practiced by a struggling society will be those that clearly serve practical purposes. You can sing as you walk beside a covered wagon, even when you're hungry, and you will walk better if you do. You can build beautiful temples with your first limited surplus, and no one, not even the person blind to beauty, will complain that you are wasting good money and time on frills.

As young Mormons early in this century began to discover the world's great artistic traditions and to compare them with the indifference or even hostility that I have described, they were often led to conclude that in any conflict between the Church and art, the Church was wrong. Many young artists, and would-be artists, simply "went back East" and left the Church, disgusted with the culture that seemed to care more about singing "Put Your Shoulder to the Wheel" than about Beethoven's Ninth Symphony. Writers such as Vardis Fisher and Bernard De Voto could not resist portraying Utah as a cultural desert, always with the implication that when religious values and artistic culture clash, it is obvious that religion is the culprit.

But the long history of warfare between various religions and various arts and the spotted history of efforts by churches to accommodate or even foster great art suggest immense complexities underlying Mormondom's present rapidly warming embrace of the arts. Great art works and great religious cultures are both delicate plants, and the moments when the highest achievements in both are harmonized seem few and far between. Most religions have been either highly selective in the arts they have fostered, or have, like the Quakers, produced little significant art of any kind. Most churches have banned at least some of the arts, as the Quakers banned music, the Baptists dancing, the Muslims all representational painting and sculpture, the English Puritans all theatrical works. What is more, even those religions, like Catholicism, that are noted for their artistic traditions have in many historical periods expressed intolerance either of entire arts or of particular works, as specific kinds of painting were banned and specific literary works put on the Index. Perhaps the most puzzling instance of all is the seemingly impoverished artistic culture of the Bible. It is for me a sobering experience, as a lifelong devotee of the arts, to run through the Bible searching for favorable references to any art. The Old Testament does speak approvingly of song, and it frequently *enacts,* in its own words, an approval of poetry. But aside from these, the arts are all graven images and devilish idols and wicked dancing. And the New Testament is—should one say "of course"?—even leaner. As Matthew Arnold noted a century ago, Hebraism did not foster the artistic consciousness and often was openly opposed to it. Yet as we all know, Hebraic culture has indeed produced, early and late, rich artistic cultures. Some of them have been able to live in harmony with religious faith, but many of them, like most modern art produced by Jewish artists, have been in open conflict with religious tradition.

In spite of this ambiguous history, most of us—at least those of us who write for or read a volume of this kind—will continue to assume that religion and art are somehow mutually supportive, and that a great religion like Mormonism should produce more great art than we have seen so far.

Surely the best art will provide the best food for the religious spirit; surely it provides the best means for the promulgation of that spirit in the world. And on the other hand, we cannot doubt that religion provides artists with the deepest, most serious, most abiding subjects and the most compelling motives for true greatness. No matter how difficult it may be to amass evidence for our belief in an ultimate harmony and a mutual support, we cannot contemplate the works of religious composers such as Bach and Stravinsky, or of religious writers like Dante, Milton, or our modern Flannery O'Connor and François Mauriac, or of the great religious painters of the Renaissance, without hoping for similar achievements in Mormon culture.

What are the obstacles? The first is the most visible, but it is perhaps the most easily overcome: Specific church doctrines sometimes will conflict with doctrines stated or implied in specific artistic enterprises. Artists by their nature develop wills of their own, and as they probe reality with their art, they express conceptions that seem unorthodox. Quarrels will result—quarrels of the kind reflected cleverly in Browning's poem about Fra Lippo Lippi. Lippi wanted to paint angels and saints and priests one way, and his employer, the Church, wanted him to paint them strictly in the service of an obvious piety. Such quarrels will never disappear, so long as the Church is vital and its artists genuinely alive. The Church will want its prophets and evangelists portrayed without warts, and the painter will want to put them in. Both sides should find it possible to accommodate, so long as both can genuinely respect their differing immediate goals. Differences need not be in themselves fatal either to art or to the Church, provided the deeper problems we are coming to are somehow overcome.

A second obstacle to producing really great art within the Church is perhaps equally superficial. The fact is that to create any major art work requires a kind of single-minded devotion, through years of discipline, that is not easily exercised in Mormon culture. We are a busy, active, social people, who always have something to do in a public way. The notion of a daily private retreat, of working single-mindedly for years on end on one project with no visible practical value, of neglecting, necessarily, many other forms of good work in the world—this notion is not exactly widespread among us. Every author, even of something so slight as this discussion I am writing now, knows that to get it done at all requires the neglect of other good things that might be done. And one always knows that the achievement might have been better if even more private time had been stolen from the world's immense demands. When we speak of great art we are speaking of "years of hours" stolen, somehow, from the public domain.

When we look at the great art produced in other religious cultures, we generally find that some kind of official sanction of sustained privacy has been its base: life in a monastery, patronage from a cardinal or pope, retreat centers, court appointments. To some slight degree the modern university serves now to provide some few Mormon artists with *some* private hours for creation. But in fact we make it hard for any artist to withdraw from us for long enough to do more than weekend painting or late-night literary composition. The hours "stolen" are stolen from more public forms of virtuous activity.

But again, this conflict can be solved, provided a more serious conflict is overcome. But it is by no means clear that it can be. I am thinking of what seems to be an almost overwhelming drive by art itself to replace religion, to become itself the only "religion" of its devotees.

As various beliefs thought to be essential to religion have been surrendered through the last three hundred years, more and more people have turned to art as the last true and unfailing value they could cling to. "The life of art" has become, for many artists since the Romantic period, something sacred—sacred in the sense that pursuit of artistic excellence has been seen as the supreme goal in life, a goal beyond question, a goal worth the sacrifice of everything else in the world. Love, honor, social obligation, personal salvation, public decency—all were considered expendable by the genius who could make great art from the ruins. (For an account of the aspiration of art to become a religion, see Jacques Barzun's *The Use and Abuse of Art.*)

When such claims are made for art, it is surely not surprising that defenders of religion respond with suspicion and even with attempts at suppression. If we define art as the entire range of "invented experiences" (in contrast, that is, to direct experience in "real" situations), then it is clear that in 1980 the conflict between art (and most "artists") and religion is at least as strong as it ever was, probably stronger. What is worse, the actual works of art produced in the name of art's worship have not on the whole been of a kind to make defenders of religion feel like offering an uncritical home to art's devotees. The attempt to create a poetry that would replace the functions of traditional religion was threatening enough when, as in Matthew Arnold's sustained effort, the poetry being offered was itself of a kind essentially compatible with religious aspirations. Arnold offered the great classics, as interpreted by a profoundly ethical criticism, and he was even willing to ban from the pantheon his own works, such as "Empedocles on Aetna," because they might do harmful things to the spirit of man. But it is hard to argue that a similar ethical integrity informs the predominant art of 1980. Our lives are filled with "art works" as lives never were before in the history of mankind. But what art works! Can anyone who samples our national fiction lists, our movie fare, our TV programs, our magazine racks, or even the offerings of our serious poets and novelists and dramatists, recommend our "artists" and their "art" as something we should cultivate? Can a religious person seriously recommend to young people today that they become "artists," when artistic success seems to be represented by everything from being a photographer for *Playboy* to writing an exploitative work like Norman Mailer's *The Executioner's Song?*

The average Mormon's experience with art works of all kinds, in this broadened sense of the term, is immeasurably greater in quantity than it was in my childhood. I suspect that the average Mormon child meets as many vicarious experiences, of the kind made by "artists," in a week as I would have met in a year. And most of them are beneath contempt, obviously and energetically opposed to every ideal the Church stands for.

How can a committed people combat such stuff? I see only four possibilities. They might attempt, like the Amish, to isolate themselves completely from the rest of American society, banning all art works except the scriptures. They might, secondly, attempt to impose a censorship program, allowing people (or trying to allow people) to see, read, or hear, only what the censors declare harmless or beneficial. They might attempt to put their energy into the harmless or "wholesome" arts like ballroom dancing, athletics, symphony orchestras that play mainly safe traditional music, hymns, and fiction with clearly recognizable inspirational messages. Or they might try to develop a great art so powerful that it would counteract, by its very strength, the shoddy culture it opposes.

The most tempting of these four possibilities is the third: development of safe "performing" arts of various kinds that all can enjoy without any deep personal commitment or cost in spiritual struggle. Such a program might "work," in one sense, if our young people were in fact isolable from the more vigorous trends of our national culture. One might even try "Osmondizing" the various popular arts, developing a "clean" version of the late night show, a pure kind of horror movie, a nice imitation of the girlie magazines. But it wouldn't work. Bland art is no defense against powerful bad art. Young Mormons are daily flooded with slick debasements of life; they watch the shoddy but vivid TV programs and commercials, and their desires are framed by such watching. They go to the movies that offer them visions of happiness that will destroy their souls. Those who read at all read Mailer and Michener and—well, take a look at the best-seller lists. The effects of such stuff simply cannot be combated either with isolation or with exhortation or with a bland, comfortable art. Powerful vicious art will drive out weak pious art every time. When people are offered a choice between *The Executioner's Song* and a Sunday School tract, many will choose Mailer, or worse, leaving only the most passive and indifferent behind.

The best hope, then, and I would not argue that it is a strong one, is to cultivate an artistic culture that will, by its nature, counteract what "the world" offers. How you do that is, as I have suggested, a mystery. But there is one element of any such culture that is to some degree in our power. Whatever else can be said about the great periods of religious art in the past, they have always occurred in conjunction with periods of great critical alertness in the "consuming public." Often that public has been small and elitist. But we cannot be satisfied unless we think of it as encompassing everyone reached by the Church.

A critical culture is a culture of people who know how to exercise their own judgment in criticizing works of art—people who do not depend on anyone else to tell them whether a work of art is good. A critical culture is a culture of "critics," a culture of those who are willing and able to judge whether a given work of art is virtuous, lovely, or of good report, or praiseworthy, and will thus know whether to seek after more things of that kind.

Too often in my experience the development of the critical spirit is identified with being "negative." Then it is rejected because to "criticize" someone is unfair, or unkind, or elitist.

Indeed it would be surprising if some readers are not now feeling uneasy. If we cultivate the critical spirit, will we not in fact cultivate a habit of negativism that will then be applied on inappropriate occasions and against matters that should be above criticism?

A few years ago I happened to mention to a young Mormon friend that I thought one of the new temples far less beautiful than our average. He at once grew angry. "All the temples are equally beautiful; their building was inspired by the Lord. How could any of them not be the best possible?" Obviously the very notion that artistic excellence is a precious and rare thing, that even sacred buildings might vary in excellence, and that a good Mormon might serve his Church by learning to distinguish the beauty, say, of the St. George Temple from the—well, fill in the blank with your least favorite Church building—such notions not only had not entered his head, but when I expressed them he thought it was a further sign of my deplorable backsliding.

It will obviously be difficult to reconcile many habits of our thought with this critical spirit that is necessary in the creation of an artistic culture. Like the American society of which it is in many ways representative, our culture has rightly stressed the equal rights of all people to equal consideration; we come from a "universalist" tradition that has tended to stress the acceptability of whatever is "the best" that each person can do, however mediocre it might be. When I gave my first two-and-one-half-minute talk in Sunday School or when I played my first clarinet solo, I was not told that they were actually terrible performances. And surely it would not have been right to tell me that the talk was dull and disorganized, the solo out of tune, shrill, and unmusical. Should not everyone be encouraged to do the best he can?

I think so. But I also know, or think I know, that high artistic culture is not made that way. High artistic culture is made by those who have learned the habits of discrimination, the habits of criticism. Great music is composed only in cultures in which many people have learned to recognize and reject mediocre music when they hear it; great literature is written only in cultures that have developed audiences who are willing to talk about differences of quality, to reward those who do best, and to "punish"—with neglect, at the least, and with painful criticism when necessary—whatever is second rate.

I said earlier that human beings can "survive" without art. But it is not at all clear that a church can survive as a great church without an art that expresses its members' highest aspirations. When every member could rightly feel that the mere act of colonizing Utah, and building homes and churches there, was a great creative act, when the art of "making" was daily practiced simply in getting the shed built before winter or the crib built before childbirth, noble lives could be led without the trappings of the other kinds of "making" I am talking about. To work on designing and building one great temple is enough to ennoble a lifetime; our problem is to find a creative purpose half so significant in our time as those acts were in theirs. And my point is that we cannot find that purpose without taking the risks entailed by it. The risks of building a critical culture are the same risks that are run by allowing free agency of any kind: Some people will make mistakes. Certain art works may prove ultimately harmful to someone. Toes will be stepped on. Controversy will develop. In the early days of the Church it sometimes seemed that every member felt he had the right to invent new doctrine; we would perhaps find, if we developed a critical culture, that every member would claim the right to praise or reject the poems and stories and paintings and statues and buildings produced around him—even if they carried some sort of official badge.

Such risks should not be minimized. Indeed, it may well be, as some outside critics assert, that the Mormon church cannot afford to encourage a critical culture because a critical culture would not only question much that is questionable, but it would "sell out" to a secular culture of the kind I have lamented above. I personally think that is a misguided fear, but it represents the real choice that must be made: Either take that risk, or do not expect to produce a great Mormon artistic culture.

Whether the old warfare between art and religion can, in this troubled century, be transformed into a mutual support, no one can say. I cannot claim to know what kinds of art might best serve Mormondom in the next century or to predict what kinds of creative energy would be released by the formation of a genuine critical culture. But it does seem as certain as such matters can ever be that the vitalizing of our artistic creation through the vitalizing of our critical culture is an essential step toward our becoming the world religion that we aspire to be.

Art and Worship: Toward a Theoretical Accommodation

Nicolas Shumway

The easiest way to avoid solving a problem is to deny that it exists. Such is the approach of those who glibly maintain that art in a Church context poses no problem for Latter-day Saints because art is one thing and Church another, that trying to meet the demands of both is serving contrary masters. Despite its enviable simplicity, such an argument has little to do with the Church as most of us know it and in the long run is better for stopping discussions than solving problems. The fact is that in today's Church, music is an essential part of worship services, each Church building is potentially an art object, visitors' centers rely heavily on visual representations, literature and theater from Jesus' parables to Shakespeare's plays are used in teaching, and Church artists and intellectuals are repeatedly asked to make contributions to the kingdom—an odd assignment if art is supposedly one thing and the Church another.

The facile bifurcation of Church and art does, however, have its attractions, for art, artists, and art lovers do indeed cause problems. I recall, for example, one accomplished conductor who, wanting to offer the best of her talent and experience to the Lord, spent many hours teaching an ambitious work to her ward choir and even organized a small orchestra for the performance. Although the choir members enjoyed the experience, her bishop said he would have found a "special" arrangement of a hymn just as satisfying, and a few people in the ward grumbled that the conductor was exploiting the members to further her own career.

Feelings were hurt on all sides, and the conductor eventually became inactive, convinced that she would never find a community in the Church. In another instance a stake leader refused to allow a gifted painter to exhibit one of his canvases in a stake art show because it portrayed nude figures. The artist intended his painting to be an allegorical representation of baptism and the resurrection with the nudity symbolizing newness and purity, but his stake leader called the work pornographic. And there is the rock musician who was hurt when told the song he wrote about his conversion was appropriate only for Church dances. Or the visitors' center guide who is fed up with all the carping about the bad art in the visitors' centers that contribute to so many conversions. Or the organist who cannot understand why such a wealthy church cannot afford more pipe organs. Or the Church architect who claims that keeping abreast of building needs precludes undue emphasis on beauty and originality. Or any one of the dozen cases all of us can think of.

Why is art such a problem? Why can't artists just get with the program and stop fussing so much? No simple answer to such questions will do, for in reality there are good reasons for a variety of opinions on the role of art in the Church; and when examined carefully, each has its merit.

Many Latter-day Saints feel art should be good for something, that is to say, it should be useful, utilitarian. Essentially a pragmatism based on mass response, the utilitarian position assumes that the value of art depends wholly on what it accomplishes. The goals of the Church may be broadly defined as the perfecting of the members and the spreading of the gospel. Consequently, if we accept the utilitarian approach, Church art can be judged in terms of those goals, and the criteria for judging art can be found in two simple questions: Does it say the right thing, and does it say it in a fashion acceptable to the greatest number of people? Or, put a different way, the message must be doctrinally correct and the medium carrying that message must communicate it effectively to as large an audience as possible. Such concepts are not compatible with any notions of value in the art object itself—art for art's sake—nor do they assume that the message should determine the medium, that the form should complement the content. Similarly, in a utilitarian framework, the artist's sincerity, skill, or sophistication count for nothing. The appropriateness of the form depends wholly on the response of the audience.

It is not uncommon for good art to be concerned with religious, moral, or social values, and the notion that such values in art somehow demean it would surely surprise artists like Dante, Michelangelo, Bach, and Dickens. The problem lies in the fact that, carried to its logical extremes, utilitarian thinking leads to formal anarchy by implying that as long as the message is acceptable to a particular audience, any form is as good as another. For example, if it is shown that rock music best communicates religious truths to a particular audience, using utilitarian criteria, there is no reason not to set gospel texts in a rock idiom. Similarly, bluegrass music, flashing neon signs, bilious billboards, garbled grammar, and Baldwin Fun Machines are all acceptable means of communicating gospel principles if the audience so warrants.

Although the above examples are extreme, a basic utilitarianism justifies in the minds of many a great deal of Church art that others find questionable. For example, many Latter-day Saint artists and art enthusiasts grumble about the sentimental didacticism of some of the visual representations in the visitors' centers, claiming that the paintings and statuary are blatantly commercial, decorative, unimaginative, and unidimensional. But their complaints usually fall on deaf ears, for in the visitors' centers many people become interested in the Church. Undoubtedly, many educated non-Mormons react as negatively to the marriage of religion and Madison Avenue as do their intellectual counterparts within the Church, but because individuals constitute a minority, those who make utilitarian policies need not take their opinions seriously.

Similarly, Church musicians frequently complain that excess concern for the common denominator also limits Church music. Our membership generally associates religion with nineteenth-century four-part harmony, and in good utilitarian fashion, Church music meets their expectations. What is associated with the truth becomes, by association, also true. For example, the predominantly middle-class respectability of the Church dictates avoidance of Nashville gospel singing but also precludes the music of Bach, Palestrina, and other great religious composers simply because most members of the Church lack the background to appreciate such music either as music or as an affirmation of Christian faith. But again, utilitarian thinking is not concerned with trained musicians, but with mass response. For similar reasons electronic organs often are preferred over pipe organs because "most people don't know the difference anyway."

If one accepts a utilitarian view of art in the kingdom and if in fact such items as visitors' center murals and nineteenth-century hymnody accomplish their purposes, there is no basis for refuting any of them. To the argument that art in the Church is seldom very good, the utilitarian can reply that it is not the Church's function to produce art, but to teach the gospel, that art has no value in the Church except as a vehicle for conveying a particular message. If it is said that the utilitarian view fails to distinguish between art and propaganda, the utilitarian may agree, but he will quickly point out that while the word *propaganda* has unpleasant connotations, there is certainly nothing wrong with using any available means of spreading the gospel. Indeed, among people with a firm sense of absolute truth, of what is right for everyone, it would be pure shock-headedness not to take advantage of so powerful a tool as the arts.

But the charge of propaganda cannot be so easily dismissed, for propaganda is a form of distortion. Irrespective of the message involved, propagandistic art always has one thing in common: Its themes are unidimensional. Good and evil are easily identified, "correct" goals—be they Plato's Republic, the communist utopia, or the peaceable kingdom of the Jehovah's Witnesses—can be reduced to slogans, and unhappiness can only be a product of nonconformity to the "truth." Indeed, the cardinal sin in propagandistic art is ambiguity; complexity and controversy, although constants of our existence and belief, have no place in the simplistic didacticism of propaganda. Consequently, denouncing a work as propaganda carries with it a charge of dishonesty—a charge that can be formulated using one of utilitarianism's basic premises, namely that the message be true. If we subscribe to the utilitarian position on Church art, we must guard against its inevitable tendency toward propaganda; that is to say, we must ask ourselves if, in fact, the artistic presentation of the Church, its doctrines, and its history is honest, or oversimplified to the point of distortion.

Most of us would reject an exclusive utilitarianism in favor of a more formalistic approach. Formalism maintains that the worth of an art object is found in itself, irrespective of any message it may convey. Furthermore, in conceptual art, literature and representational painting for example, formalists argue that form and content are inseparable, that neither can be altered without affecting the other. Those who consider the gospel message the most important thing in their lives intuitively sense that the medium should be appropriate to the message, that the form should be worthy of the content. There is little question that the Mormon pioneers felt this way; their buildings, complete with carved wood, stained glass, and pipe organs, reflect a desire to express their faith through their best talents, training, and effort. In today's Church, formalist thinking contributes to the injunction against rock and popular music in sacrament meetings, even when the texts are doctrinally inoffensive. On the other hand, it is also a formalist orientation that discourages the use of brass instruments in worship services—as if themes such as the Resurrection or St. John's seven seals could be announced on a flute or violin.

The notion that, beyond being appropriate, the form should be *worthy* of the message implies a hierarchy of formal properties, which is to say that just as certain messages are better than others, so should the forms conveying those messages be better than others. But deciding which forms are better is a tricky matter since to some degree the apprehension and appreciation of beauty depend on personal and intuitive criteria. For centuries, some critical theorists have argued that beauty and worth in art are ultimately unanalyzable properties and that it is therefore impossible to speak with any kind of authority on matters of taste. For example, if one person says he likes a particular painting and another disagrees, it is entirely probable that both are telling the truth about their personal feelings, but neither is saying anything objectively verifiable about the painting.

Most of us, however, would reject the notion that one person's opinion on the worth of an art object is necessarily as good as anyone else's: TV sitcoms are not Shakespeare, regardless of who likes them. We often hear people say, "I don't know anything about art, but I know what I like." Such statements, according to formalists, should not go unchallenged, for frequently they are used to justify intellectual laziness. A person need not be a composer or poet to appreciate fine music or good literature, and informed appreciation is clearly within the realm of anyone willing to make the effort. Wallowing in one's ignorance would be intolerable in any other field of practical or spiritual endeavor. We would never accept a statement like, "I don't know anything about the scriptures, but I know what I believe." Such an attitude is no more tolerable in the arts. Particularly questionable is the notion that Church members can discern the Lord's attitude toward art in the Church while admitting ignorance of the arts themselves. Section nine of the Doctrine and Covenants clearly indicates the futility of calling on the Spirit of the Lord in ignorance. Formalists argue that in art, as in any other field of endeavor, people who have talent, training, and experience are better qualified to evaluate it and make policy regarding it than those unable to make informed observations. Furthermore, an informed opinion is more than a personal reaction because one can also consider the opinions of other critics as well as the so-called judgment of time. In addition, by analyzing such elements as unity, complexity, and intensity, an educated viewer or listener can find ample ground for understanding and judging a particular piece somewhat objectively. Indeed, it is quite possible for such a person, utilizing experience, analysis, and study, to recognize the artistic worth of a work without particularly liking it.

People informed in artistic matters frequently find the utilitarian focus of some of the art in the Church offensive. Subscribing to basic formalist doctrines, they feel that form and content are inseparable and that when the content is of such transcendent importance as the gospel, it deserves a form equally sublime, a form that like all great art speaks in a particularly firm voice to its own generation and to all generations. The gospel, according to such people, is designed to satisfy not only the lowest common denominator, but to contain the highest aspirations of the human spirit. The fact that much of the Bible is poetry and drama testifies that religious experiences often demand artistic expression. Joseph Smith was particularly aware of the power expression acquires when form complements content. The Prophet's discourses exhibit a constant preoccupation with eloquence. Joseph Smith was not a man of great schooling, but he believed in his work, and when he was teaching the gospel, he used the best language at his disposal. Totally absent in this man of the frontier is the studied folksiness so tediously present in many of today's speakers.

It is precisely because of this tight relationship between form and content that Latter-day Saint artists and connoisseurs find some Church practices in art so frustrating. There is little question but that visitors' center paintings and temple murals are useful illustrations, but some Latter-day Saint artists feel that the themes involved deserve more formal refinement. Similarly, many musicians and writers feel that the sing-song melodies, monotonous harmonizations, skip-along rhythms, and humdrum verse of some of our hymns, not to mention the soft-rock monotony of *Saturday's Warrior* and its clones, hardly reflect the highest artistic accomplishments of the human spirit that should accompany the gospel message. It is no secret that the Church frequently employs nonmember painters to paint the murals found in visitors' centers, supposedly because Mormon artists are uncooperative, temperamental, and too interested in the glory of the world to render service to the Church. Perhaps the fact is that many Latter-day Saint artists believe too strongly both in the Church and in their art to participate in the seeming commercialization of the gospel message. The non-Mormon has no such scruples; he paints what he is paid to paint, and he sees little difference between selling Mormonism and selling deodorant.

Like the utilitarians, the talented and educated elite (or formalists as I have somewhat arbitrarily called them here) defend themselves well; but despite the seeming theoretical solidity of their position, we must consider yet another view of art in the Church. Church membership consists no more of just a mass audience than it does of just an educated few. Also fundamentally vital in the gospel is the individual, the one. Indeed, perhaps only in God's kingdom can the paradox be maintained that finds one life equal to all lives, as is shown in Jesus' parable of the one and the ninety and nine. It is in this light that we must consider a third approach to art in the Church: art as expression.

The expressionist viewpoint holds that art is fundamentally an expression of an individual human emotion, a "spontaneous overflow of powerful feelings," if we may borrow from Wordsworth's definition of poetry. The formal features of the art object itself are merely means employed by the artist to represent his feelings. So defined, the art object serves at least two functions. First, in its creation, the artist is in effect exploring his feelings, trying to understand and give voice to the emotions that demand expression. In this sense art becomes a powerful means of soul-probing introspection. Second, the art object can stimulate the same sort of self-inquiry in the percipient. Although expressionist theory does not usually include the feelings art may evoke in its audience, we must conclude (if such notions as creative, purposeful reading, listening, or viewing have any validity) that the audience can participate in the expressive experience.

Perhaps the chief difficulty with expressionist theory is that it supplies no objective evaluative criteria; according to its framework, artistic worth depends wholly on standards of sincerity and personal significance not unlike one's attempts to bear testimony. No one imbued with any spirit of charity would condemn another member's efforts to bear a testimony, no matter how clumsy or incomprehensible that testimony might sound. During a testimony meeting, each member properly suspends judgment and accepts the attempts of others to communicate what is for each individual a private and often agonizingly inexpressive knowledge. A sincere work of art should be regarded as a testimony borne in the language the artist finds most natural and expressive. And just as we would scarcely dare condemn a testimony borne in a language we do not understand or in speech characterized by accent and intonations different from our own, so we must refuse to condemn the work of art that similarly seeks to express the religious experience or vision of a particular individual. To condemn a genuinely sincere and personally meaningful art object because it is not obviously didactic, moralistic, or formally perfect is to condemn the artist. Of course, if we confine ourselves to expressionist theory, neither can it be condemned for being simplistic, incomprehensible, perverted, or mad. In an expressive framework, the artist's intentions and feelings demand highest priority—a position not unlike Paul's affirmation that it is by faith that we are judged, by the spirit and not the letter. The irksome inconclusiveness of expressionist theory accounts for the claim that expressionism is more a psychology of art than a theory of art. It is certainly true that no great artist has ever been exclusively expressionist; even the most devout expressionist must deal with formal problems (e.g., language, colors, shapes, and harmonies) in objectivizing his emotions. Nonetheless, in a Church where individual feelings are important, the central tenets of the expressionist position cannot be ignored.

In our discussion we have looked at three major approaches to art and discussed briefly how each relates to the problem of art in the Church. The fact that there are powerful arguments against supporting any particular viewpoint in all cases leads us to what may have been an obvious conclusion from the beginning: Art in the Church exists for different reasons, and the Church cannot possibly satisfy all of the people all of the time. There is, however, no rational excuse for attitudes that preclude satisfying all groups some of the time, nor is there any justification for ignoring the artistic needs of Church members who are not part of the invisible—and probably nonexistent—majority. Our religious health is not determined by how many people we can exclude, but rather by how many we can accept. In such an ambience of tolerance it is likely that the Church can better fulfill its mission, both to the individual and to the world, and that the solid artistic traditions begun by the early Mormons may someday reach fruition.

Church members would do well to learn about the creation of great religious art in the past. Pope Julius and Michelangelo are almost as famous for their disagreements as for their accomplishments, but at no time did Julius want anyone but Michelangelo to paint the Sistine ceiling. As a result, in that immortal work we find traces of each of the viewpoints discussed here: It is utilitarian in its portrayal of religious truths, formalist in its artistic conception, and expressive of the personal vision of a great individual artist. There were no doubt dozens of painters like today's commercial artists who would have painted exactly what Julius wanted the first time around. But because of the Pope's tolerance and willingness to strive with genuine talent, the Sistine Chapel contains one of the masterpieces of Christian art. Given the proper combination of tolerance, talent, and faith, Mormondom may someday produce a work equally moving that reflects our religious experience. In the process we can make life richer for all of us by recognizing that the Church is big enough, strong enough, and mature enough to accommodate several points of view.

The Mormon Sacred
and the Mormon Profane:
An Aesthetic Dilemma

Karen Lynn

Since the early years of Mormon history, Church leaders appear to
have granted the arts a legitimate place. Brigham Young, for example, surprised the American public by endorsing dance and drama. Mormons may find themselves, of course, objecting to the
content of particular works or trends—the decadent subject matter
of R-rated films, or the dangers of morally permissive rock lyrics—
but these objections have always been aimed at content rather
than at the artistic forms themselves. Even the early warnings
against novel-reading from such leaders as Brigham Young and
George Q. Cannon were in fact objections to particular content,
not to narrative or fictional forms. The genre itself was not suspect.[1] For Mormons, then, the only issue in the enjoyment and
creation of art has been one of discrimination, of determining
which works of fiction, or of any other artistic form, are wholesome and refining.

Of course, a pioneering society understandably holds the arts
to be principally ornamental, and members of the Church during
the early decades naturally saw survival as their primary task. Even
so, a few of the pioneer Saints were preoccupied with an anxiety
that besets every marginal society: the fear of being seen as un-
couth, unlettered, and uncreative, of being dismissed by the larger
society as cultural barbarians. Undoubtedly the paradox was (and
perhaps still is) deeply disturbing: While the Mormons knew
themselves to be uniquely and divinely chosen as vessels of heavenly revelation, it was the artists of the majority culture who still

44

spoke for the admiration of the world, who spoke, somehow, with the voice of God. All too aware that some visitors to Salt Lake City had described the Mormons as "grossly illiterate ... very backward and ignorant when compared with other dwellers on the American continent,"[2] many of the Saints longed to be recognized, not only as being educated in the mainstream, but also as manifesting their unique status as the divinely chosen people through impressive artistic performances. Statements from the First Presidency year after year reflect their conviction that the condescending, mocking Gentile world was slowly being forced to change its opinion: "A tour of the Tabernacle Choir to New York and other cities of the East has opened the eyes of hundreds of thousands of our fellow citizens to the fact that the 'Mormons' are not the ignorant, uncultivated people supposed, but are an intelligent part of the great human family."[3] "We are rapidly coming to the front in music, art, science, law, and literature, and all this is but a galaxy of stars that in the future as glowing suns will shine with such lustre that Utah will be the admiration of the world."[4] And early Church periodicals, establishing a practice that continues to this day, printed many laudatory accounts of Mormon artists and the recognition they had received.[5] Mormons, then, have been unequivocally anxious to prove themselves in the arts, to understand and adapt the mainstream cultural givens, and to contribute to that stream as artists and as Mormons. Individual members of the Church have indeed distinguished themselves according to high artistic standards in every area of the fine arts, and the pride of the LDS community in these artists is understandable.

Nevertheless, despite these remarkable contributions, and despite the many authoritative statements endorsing study and appreciation of the arts and encouraging artistic creativity, it is my conviction that the Mormon community is at the very least indifferent toward the arts. Discrimination between first-rate and inferior art according to aesthetic standards is taxing, abstract, and sometimes awkward; it is easier and more agreeable to be satisfied with praiseworthy content, without reference to significant form.

The conviction that Mormons prefer to relegate genuine artistic involvement to the comfortable margins of life is an intuitive one, not capable of any direct proof. It derives simply from the sense that Mormons—anxious to prove themselves possessors of superior health, superior families, superior organization, and superior doctrine—wish merely to possess an array of genteel successes to complement successes of other kinds. The mere existence of

46

murals and musicals, the sheer number of them, is taken as proof of the Mormon commitment to the arts. Yet all this "artistic" activity without true artistic result is the very thing that brings into doubt the genuineness of that commitment.

Furthermore, social or didactic or proselyting motives,[6] rather than primarily aesthetic ones, often initiate or justify whatever interest in the arts the Mormon community may have. A child studies music so that he will have a hobby to keep him out of mischief; a family decorates a den with photographs of temples so that the children will be reminded of the importance of temple marriage; a Relief Society studies the literature of foreign lands in order to establish bonds of worldwide sisterhood.[7] The fine arts fit in where they can. No niche in Mormon life is reserved for them; the arts are not the exclusive answer to any particular Mormon longing. Nor are they the unique bread that will satisfy a particular Mormon hunger.

These remarks will assume that the formal position of the Church toward the arts—an endorsement of the forms but with reservations concerning the content—does not reflect the underlying attitudes of the Mormon community. Notwithstanding our repeated claims, I feel that the Mormon attitude toward the arts goes beyond simple indifference. In fact, the very forms of art, no matter how unobjectionable the content, are somehow suspect and unwelcome.

Almost any member of the Mormon church who senses these misgivings of the community regarding the arts can offer suggestions as to their cause. The reasons cited are many, and are frequently repeated: Art must have a tragic dimension, and the faith of Mormons in divine justice leaves them no room ultimately to believe in tragedy; Mormons are so concerned with well-roundedness that the single-minded dedication necessary to first-rate artistic achievement is impossible; Mormons are practical, and the arts usually cannot be eaten and hardly ever can be turned to financial profit; Mormons are so busy that the arts are just peripheral; Mormons are suspicious of the emotions, and the emotional dimension of the arts therefore renders them suspicious; Mormons will be held accountable for so many important things—ritual, service, right belief, missionary work—that nothing falling outside the direct pursuit of these goals is a legitimate concern.

To some degree, all these reasons are undoubtedly valid. Yet some may themselves have more abstract, more fundamental causes. These remarks will deal with two such abstract causes, two realities of Latter-day Saint culture that prevent Mormons from giving uninhibited endorsement even to the forms of art or to the creative act. For these two reasons, and perhaps for a host of others, the arts cannot be central to Mormon life no matter how many times we may claim otherwise. Both points refer principally to literary creation, but implications for other artistic disciplines follow from the literary examples.[8]

Scriptural Sufficiency and Mormon Creativity

The sacred texts of Mormonism—the standard works—are held by Mormons to be complete and immutable. They are crucial, holy artifacts, artifacts realized as language. Therefore they are the ultimate, the *sine qua non,* of theology and admonition. They are, to underline the point once again, definitive, complete, and perfect—perfect in the sense of the Latin *per fectus,* completely made. What, then, is the role of someone who wishes to write something in addition to these texts? The LDS church, as already stated, has never denounced the artist as heretical simply because he is an artist, and in no direct way does the writer raise the specter of heresy simply by creating a story or a poem. Yet the sacred texts cast their shadow, standing as an inimitable comparative standard and demanding that certain assumptions be made about any subsequent act of creativity, particularly verbal creativity.

What, then, are the possible relationships of a present-day author to these texts? Obviously, he cannot presume to add further volumes to the formal set of scripture. But Mormonism, like many other religions, depends upon modern commentary to illuminate the holy teachings and redefine them for each generation. Isn't it possible that the Latter-day Saints could create a body of literature to reflect back on the sacred writings, exploring and validating them for the enlightenment of the modern community? Though the sacred writings are complete and definitive, couldn't literature be justified as a sort of footnote to the standard works, a secondary apparatus to aid in the crucial understanding of eternal truths? Our insistence upon deriving a moral from each work of literature, or upon imposing our own moral and didactic framework upon that literature, shows a tendency in this direction already.

The fact is, however, that Mormonism does not ask its novelists and poets to interpret and promulgate scriptural truths; the Brethren alone have this task. Because the words of our leaders are in some sense accorded the status of scripture, it is these words that are the ongoing prescriptive set, a gloss defining the modern relevance of the holy words. The Brethren offer commentary through general conference addresses, through books, and through Church periodicals. Thus, because the texts are complete, it is sacrilege to ornament them or to add to them; and because the Brethren are divinely called as stewards over the modern relevance of the text, it is sacrilege for anyone else to expound upon them.[9]

A debate concerning the aesthetic value of a piece of literature, or even concerning its wholesomeness, at least begins with the assumption that literature of some sort deserves to exist. Yet such debates in the Mormon community may actually disguise the true issue: whether artistic creation, particularly the act of writing, is a prideful, wrong-minded replication of the already-completed, divine act of perfect verbal creation, an irreverent suggestion that man-made narrative or rhetoric should vie with the Divine Word for the attention of the faithful. The Mormon artist cannot defend his writings as an expansion or extrapolation growing out of the sacred texts, because he has not been called to offer such commentary; and he cannot defend the creation of totally new works without betraying his own attitudes toward the ostensible completeness of the sacred texts. Private creation is not a means to truth, nor even an acceptable means to the restatement and promulgation of established truth. Thus, it *is* the form of the art, the fact that it was written at all, and not just an occasional problem with content, that is troublesome. The status of the scriptures in the Mormon community works against an unequivocal endorsement of subsequent creativity.

The Disallowing of Perplexity

The second reason I am going to suggest for the Mormon attitude toward the arts is also related to the notion of completeness. Mormonism offers its members all they need: perfect scriptures, the gospel in its fullness, a prophet to provide answers to contemporary problems. The writings (with their ongoing prescriptive gloss) are sufficient, establishing the purpose of life, its right conduct, and its ultimate justice. Then why would a Mormon whose belief is strong ever feel despair? Why, in fact, would he even feel perplexed? Bleakness and confusion are not acceptable; if a complete set of answers and instructions is available, then a confused person must assume all responsibility for his own unhappy state. If he only believed and understood, he would realize that in the writings and leadership of the Church he has all he needs for his satisfaction and peace of mind.

This is not to say that the LDS church denies the reality of opposition and struggle. We acknowledge that perplexity will be part of the experience of every human. But perplexity and struggle, we claim, characterize only the natural man; those who put him off will become serene and clear eyed. The godly, faithful life cannot be a life of unhappiness and confusion. So we insist on success stories and refuse to accommodate stories of defeat, or even stories of righteous struggle unless these stories end by affirming a highly predictable and rather simple role for deity.

Yet this concept of a just, comprehensible, predictable God, a thoroughly known God whose universe is carefully designed and ordered and whose preferences and judgments are clearly established, is exactly the concept that receded when modern modes of fiction began to develop. As the Mexican writer Carlos Fuentes has said, significant fiction must acknowledge that the struggle of human existence is "between equally legitimate forces, forces that together represent a moral dilemma that can only be transcended by embracing the moral conflict of its antagonist."[10] To a sensitive writer of fiction, tension and irresolution are not preliminary or secondary; they are inherent in the human condition, as real and everlasting as any other part of life, and they must be reflected and reconciled in any work that seeks to deal with life in a meaningful way. Yet the Mormon artist is finally expected to deny these darker realities, to show them as ultimately invalid in a true vision of life, and therefore to offer what Fuentes would probably include among the works he characterizes as "the illegible palimpsest of barren white writing on a white wall ... perfectly determined ... optimistic, success-nurtured, pragmatic."[11]

Thus the fact is that, unfortunately for the Mormon artist, the admission of perplexity, like the act of writing itself, calls into question the completeness of his sacred texts. This problem is more than just a matter of the impossibility of an ultimately tragic existence in a perfectly just universe; writers such as Shakespeare, Tolstoy, Dickens, and Cervantes have seen the universe as essentially just, and yet have given human confusion and perplexity a place in that universe. But Mormonism goes further, insisting that an unhappy person is by definition blameworthy, because he has not yet learned, or has not yet accepted, all the truths available to him so that he can make right choices and thereby attain happiness. And the most unacceptable hypothesis of all would be that sincere and praiseworthy impulses could themselves be the ones that bring disaster, as they do for Antigone and Don Quixote, for example.

The implications for the writer, and for the other artists as well, are all too evident. It is not the solved problem or (as Tolstoy reminds us) the happy family that usually holds interest for writer and reader. Nevertheless, the Mormon artist finds himself a member of a community that tolerates none but the most simplistic treatments of unhappiness, depression, confusion, and frustration. If the artist describes trials, these must be the trials of a wicked, faithless, or unwise person, one who deserves whatever suffering he meets; and preferably, the trials must precede that moment that calls for the writer's true emphasis—the moment when his protagonist understands that none of his trials were real.

Thus Mormonism has always gone on record as welcoming the arts, with certain reservations about content. Yet it may be that our claim to a perfect set of sacred writings and perfect on-going counsel, and our belief in the sufficiency of our theology generally, tell all artists that in the light of the full Latter-day truth their work is superfluous. It may be that the arts will achieve legitimacy if, and only if, the faith is seriously threatened.[12] Art would then reinforce what faith had lost. Greek drama, after all, flourished only after the gods were dead, and Jewish writers stepped forth to claim Nobel prizes only after they had left orthodoxy far behind. But until that hypothetical time, beauty for the Mormon community will be defined, not in terms of a fine artistic creation, but in terms of the good deed or the willing act of obedience. Except in its most accessible and moralistic forms, art, in the minds of most Mormons, will continue to be suspected of blocking the light from the temple windows. In spite of how strongly we may wish to convince ourselves otherwise, only the most superficial resolutions of this conflict are now open to us.

Notes

1. One of George Q. Cannon's indictments of the novel appeared on 1 September 1858 in a San Francisco newspaper called the *Western Standard:* "The injury which is done to both men and women by their perusal of works of fiction ... is much greater than many, probably, of this people are aware of. The fascination is so strong, the excitement ... so pleasurable, that many en-

tirely overlook the evils consequent thereupon." The problems he goes on to cite, however, are those of popular, second-rate fiction: "The counterparts of their heroes and heroines are never to be found in the world ... the incidents ... are unnatural, and grossly improbable exaggerations. ... [The novels give] incorrect views of the world." The issue, obviously, is one of content, not the novel form; and in fact the novel form (with many of its popular cliches intact) was turned by the Church to its own uses. To cite one example: "A Boy's Love: A Man's Devotion," a long short story (no author given) was published in *Eventful Narratives: The Thirteenth Book of the Faith-Promoting Series,* by the Juvenile Instructor Office in 1887. In this story the childhood sweethearts Emeline Stewart and William Anderson join the Church in New England and brave many adventures together as husband and wife until many years later she heroically accepts his death in Nauvoo. The work itself includes some literary judgments. An old preacher announces "that his text will be from one of the great poets: and the congregation bent with horror to hear what dreadful thing he next would utter. Even into this remote corner of the New World had penetrated the fame of the irreverent poet lord, 'Childe Harold,' and even the very name of poet brought with it an oppressive sense of sin." Fortunately, the preacher quotes instead from Milton's "On the Morning of Christ's Nativity." But later, when William is buying a gift for Emeline and is disappointed not to find the volume of Milton he wishes, he realizes his folly and buys a Bible for her instead: "Why do I seek the modern poet who sang of Jesus? The book which tells all we know of Him, I am sure is easier got." Holy poetry is better than profane, but the scriptures can replace poetry altogether.

2. W. F. Rae, *Westward By Rail: A Journey to San Francisco and Back and a Visit to the Mormons,* 2d ed. (London: Longmans, Green, and Co., 1871), pp. 137, 180.

3. Christmas Message from the First Presidency, *Deseret News,* 16 December 1911. In James R. Clark, ed., *Messages of the First Presidency of the Church of Jesus Christ of Latter-day Saints* (Salt Lake City: Bookcraft, 1970), vol. 4, p. 255.

4. Christmas Message from the First Presidency, *Deseret News,* 16 December 1916. In Clark, vol. 5, p. 46.

5. For a description of these accounts, see James L. Haseltine, *One Hundred Years of Utah Painting* (Salt Lake City: The Salt Lake Art Center, 1965), pp. 31 ff.

6. For a discussion of the Church's preference for "community" or "group" arts, see James L. Haseltine, "Mormons and the Visual Arts," *Dialogue: A Journal of Mormon Thought* 1, no. 2 (Summer 1966): 18–19.

7. The question of the changing focus of the Relief Society manual–its presentation of increasingly nonaesthetic objectives to justify the study of literature and the other arts–is treated by Cheryll Lynn May in "Charitable Sisters," *Mormon Sisters,* ed. Claudia L. Bushman (Cambridge: Emmaline Press, 1976), pp. 225–39.

8. I would like to acknowledge the help of Seth Wolitz of the Department of Comparative Literature at the University of Texas at San Antonio, whose conversation and suggestions were vital to my discussion entitled "Scriptural Suffi-

ciency and Mormon Creativity"; and also the help of Joseph Jarvis, a former student now enrolled at the University of Utah, who has generously allowed me to read his article in progress, "The Literary Nature of Mormon Spirituality." This article was of great benefit to me in my discussion, "The Disallowing of Perplexity."

9. The existence of this ongoing commentary may seem to suggest that the Church membership does not hold the divine writings to be complete and self-contained. But this commentary merely justifies or reinterprets the original writings, without ever presuming to take its place beside them or to undermine their uniqueness. This single, approved channel of commentary provides only an overlay or a supplement, without anything like the status of the original, sacred texts. Some might object that Catholics too consider that their scriptures are complete; they have had a Bible, and yet their creativity does not seem to have been undermined. I would suggest that in traditional Christianity the scriptures have in fact not played anything like the role they do for Mormons. The sacraments, not the writings, have been the framework for the Christian population, and the sacraments are not narrative or expository or rhetorical in the same way. The act of writing would not, therefore, be presumptuous repetition and would not in fact run the same danger of substituting for or subverting a written word familiar and sacred to all members of the community. The mass, too, is a sacred text, but the mass has inspired *musical* creativity, additions and variations that surround and enhance the established text rather than competing with it, and *visual* creativity, art works that illustrate the text without overshadowing its word. These are important differences.

10. Carlos Fuentes, "Central and Eccentric Writing," in *Latin-American Literature Today,* ed. Anne Fremantle (New York: New American Library, 1977), p. 138.

11. Fuentes, p. 138.

12. In a discussion of Boccaccio's *Decameron,* Giuseppe Mazzotta has remarked that literature is "the negation of prophecy, its mockery. In a sense, literature seems to be possible precisely when prophecy fails or to indicate the failure of prophecy." "The *Decameron:* The Marginality of Literature," *University of Toronto Quarterly,* 42 (Fall 1972): 79.

The Relevance
of Literature:
A Mormon Viewpoint*

Edward L. Hart

Some time ago, in *Brigham Young University Studies,* I published
an article about Japanese and English poetry; I ended it with the
statement that poetry in both languages carries the hallmark
"Made on Earth by Man." A week or so later I received a letter
from a member of the Church in California. He had read my article, and noting my interest in Japanese things he sent me a paper
written by his son on the history of the Mormon church in Japan,
which I was very happy to get because I have a deep and continuing interest in everything Japanese. His letter, however, concluded with the statement that the paper he was sending me
stressed "Made on Earth by God."

For a long time I considered the tone of the letter. I decided
finally that my correspondent had intended merely to find a graceful transition from my article to the one he was sending, that he
had not meant his statement as a rebuke. But the possibility of
this latter interpretation stuck in my mind. What if he had meant
to say that my emphasis on the creative works of man was a mis-
application of effort, perhaps even almost a blasphemy to direct
any effort away from the praising of God? Regardless of whether
the question had been intentional, it had arisen. And any question
that can be asked, demands an answer and poses a challenge, just
as to a mountain climber the mere presence of a mountain is the

---

*Reprinted, by permission, from *Dialogue: A Journal of Mormon Thought* 5, no.
2 (1970):121–25.

challenge. I continued to turn the matter over in my mind, and my thoughts here are largely the result of ideas that began to assemble themselves in response to the question. They become, in effect, a kind of justification for my life's work.

The things we call art are, by definition, the works of man, called thus to distinguish them from nature. People have, historically, valued art because of the very fact that, having passed through the mind of a man, it becomes a human interpretation of an object, an idea, or an event. In defense of this activity, I first asked myself the question: Is there anything in specifically Mormon beliefs that would preclude artistic pursuits on the part of Church members? Or from a more positive position, an even better question: Are there specific Mormon beliefs that contribute to a justification of a career in the arts?

In approaching these questions, I felt I should be quite basic, and I could find nothing more basic than the Mormon concept of God: a God who not only loves his children as does an earthly father but who is, as well, their literal spiritual father. Proceeding from this, I asked: What kind of an earthly father is jealous of his children's accomplishments and advances or is wrathful if they do something worthwhile on their own? Is our Father in Heaven, then, likely to be angered at his children's presumptuousness if they become capable of creative thought or action and growth toward understanding? Perhaps the best answer is another question: Isn't every accomplishment of a man likely to be the occasion of his Father's rejoicing? One would certainly have to go to some other religion than Mormonism to find a concept of a god (not the loving Father) who frowns upon all the efforts of man, dismissing them with haughtiness as puny and insignificant.

Related to the Mormon concept of God is the Mormon explanation of why man is on earth to begin with. We do not see ourselves as mere pawns and playthings at the mercy of the caprices of a higher being; rather, we see ourselves and God together working in harmony with irrevocable law. We are here to undergo the experience of mortality in order to learn what that experience has to teach; and we are to undergo that experience not only that we might suffer, but that we might find joy. Most of the rest that I have to say will be an exploration of the ways in which art (or specifically literature from now on) contributes to man's joy. And lest my statement about finding joy in literature mislead you into thinking I am going to approach the subject from the point of view of how it pretties up life, let me say immediately that I am not. I wish, in short, to look at literature not as decoration, but as a meaningful and functional part of life itself.

I want to begin looking for the ways in which literature contributes to joy by asking what joy is and how we come by it. For this purpose, I shall omit here the approaches to this subject that are familiar in a theological framework, although doing this is deceptive since our theology informs us that there is no clear and distinct separation between spiritual and temporal meanings. But this fact itself imposes an even greater responsibility to examine things on the path along which we are going, as being a trail that is less well explored than others.

If we assume that man's purpose on earth is to fulfill in reality all the potential that he had when he came here, then joy must be the gauge, as well as the reward, of our approach to fulfillment. The problem for man, thus, is to become that which he is capable of becoming. Literature is one way of becoming. I do not claim that it is the only way, nor even that it is at all times the best way: only that it is one way and a good way. Writing is one means that an author possesses to become himself, and he can become that self only by writing. Would Shakespeare be Shakespeare if he had written no plays? Would Milton have been Milton if he had not written *Paradise Lost* and *Paradise Regained?* Shakespeare became Shakespeare and Milton became Milton only as they realized their potential for creating their various works. By the same reasoning, we who have not yet completed our life's works are not ourselves yet. You are not you yet; you are still in the process of becoming you, and you will not be you until you have made those things and done those things which, when they are made and done, will define you to yourselves and to the world. Nothing but discovering and being that self will bring joy. A person who feels that he has within himself a talent that lies undeveloped, a seed that has never burst through its husk and grown, a light that is hidden under a bushel—such a person has not become his complete self and will feel incomplete or crippled in soul and therefore deprived of joy. And man is that he might have joy.

The myths and the literatures of the world are full of the symbols of man's search for himself. In the Egyptian myth of Osiris, Isis must go in search of the dismembered parts of his body and put them together to make him whole. Most of the voyage stories involve travels in search of self: such were the voyages of Odysseus, of Huckleberry Finn, of Marlow into the Heart of Darkness—painstakingly selecting and interpreting scattered fragments of life and putting them together to make them form a whole picture. In this manner, literature (or art in general) is a close ally of religion in that both attempt to synthesize the disparate experiences of life into a unified whole. If this synthesis does not take place, a man is not a whole person, but a conglomeration of unclassified odds and ends, incomplete and unhappy.

Fortunately for men, the force that drives them to become themselves, to become one, is a strong force. It is, in my opinion, even stronger than the desire for self-preservation; and this opinion is demonstrable, for instance, in the life of someone like Joseph Smith, who chose to maintain the wholeness and integrity of his being even at the expense of life itself. This force that urges one to maintain or to attain his wholeness is, it seems to me, the source that we must turn to for an explanation of man's creative efforts. "This ache for being is the ultimate hunger," wrote D. H. Lawrence.[1]

Various explanations have been set forth as to why man creates art. W. H. Auden once said, for instance, that the artist is a misfit and that it is this that keeps him at his proper trade, which he might otherwise abandon.[2] If he were to find contentment, he would no longer utter the cry of anguish that becomes art. Aristotle introduced the therapeutic justification, which has been considerably amplified by present-day critics to include other types of therapy as well as catharsis. From this viewpoint, art is seen as the letting out of poisonous evils either from the mind of the writer or of the reader, or both. It has always seemed to me, however, that these and other similar theories leave a lot unexplained, though they have an obvious but nevertheless limited validity. I suspect that the greatest practitioners of literary art in English— Shakespeare, Chaucer, and Milton, for instance—were pushed into writing by something deeper, the necessity to become themselves, to synthesize their worlds of experience into meaningful wholes, and that there was no other way for them to do this than by writing their works. I believe that the explanation of art as the search for being can be extended to all manifestations of art, and that it is the only theory that explains all such phenomena satisfactorily.

Even on the most primitive level, human beings must reach, through art, toward some form of being beyond the requirements for survival. An Indian blanket is no warmer because of the pattern woven into it. And no matter what the explanation of how it came to be put there (such as ritual significance) the effect is the realization of a richer being on the part of the person who uses it. Quite obviously, people in the most straitened circumstances can do something creative to their surroundings, even students living on meager means. The common things a person chooses to have around him, from saltshakers to cars, create an environment which is either an emanation of himself or alien to his being. Every person has to be an artist in order to live well. The subtle things over which one has a choice in his environment are far more important to his well-being and growth than are those things over which he has no control. Why bring ugliness into daily life in the form of a glass, and have to look at it and handle it every day, just because peanut butter came in it? Why let dishonesty creep into the world in the form of things that pretend to be something they are not: of boards masquerading as bricks, for instance? These things are corruptions that we do not have to tolerate. If we do tolerate them, and if we live among them long enough, we cannot help participating in their sham.

Thus it seems to me that being honest is a rule of life that extends to literature, and it is the first rule a person must follow if he is going to search for his true being either in his own writings or in the writings of others. Dishonesty in writing is the worst kind of perjury, because here a person is lying to himself about himself. The results, in terms of craftsmanship, appear in many forms. Sentimentality, false figures of speech, irrelevant rhythms, all are distortions of the truth about life. If a person is basically honest and has any kind of sensitivity to language, he has a pretty good chance of discovering something worthwhile in his attempt to say what he thinks; but if he is not basically honest, no amount of skill in craftsmanship can cover the deficiency.

So we should by all means write. And we should not worry about writing about our own experiences since all writers draw upon their own experiences. It is often only through writing about something that has happened to us that we find what it means; and we can find what the experience means in writing only by placing it in some kind of position where we are forced to look at it objectively, as though it were happening to someone else. If the writer can do this, he can often see the relevance of an isolated experience to a total picture of life. In this way he has gathered up a fragment and put it into place in a way that will make his being more complete and whole. Without the effort at composition, a fragment of experience might have lain forever detached and meaningless. More often than not the writer, again assuming that he is proceeding' honestly, does not know how the pieces fit together until he is through. If a writer discovers nothing in the course of his composing, it is not likely that he will startle any readers with the suddenness of a discovery.

If writing is a means of achieving being, so also is reading. We cannot hope to achieve in one short lifetime all possible discoveries by means of our own writing. Fortunately, if another writer has been honest also, in his approach to his writing, we may well learn from him how to put scattered, meaningless pieces together to make whole patterns. In the process, we are likely to learn to extend sympathies toward those to whom our sympathies might not flow of their own accord. Thus the range of our understanding is extended. The closeness of literature to religion seems at this point to be quite apparent. If we are to do unto others as we would have them do unto us, we must first have the capacity to imagine what it would be like to have it done to us. Is it really possible to live Christianity, to put oneself in the place of another, without this imaginative capacity? And is not anything—literature, for instance—that extends our imaginative capacity, therefore of the utmost relevance to Christianity? Remember that when Jesus himself was on earth he taught most characteristically by means of the literary device known as the parable, not by means of an abstract philosophy or theology. In an age of unrest, mistrust, hatred, and alienation, anything that produces sympathy, understanding, and accord must be given a high priority as far as relevance is concerned.

Nor need we fear that we are displeasing Deity if we attempt to create something on our own. We stand condemned for failure to use our talents if we do not. Surely a people who see themselves as eventually organizing and peopling worlds will not object to beginning the apprenticeship here on earth. From this point of view, everything that man accomplishes helps bring to pass God's work. The stamp on a work of art, "Made on Earth by Man," is, therefore, one that needs no apology, if it is done honestly and well, since it tends also to the glorification of God.

Notes

1. From "Manifesto," fourth poem from the end of *Look! We have Come Through!* (New York: B. W. Huebsch, Inc., 1920), p. 145.

2. For a discussion of this see Robert B. Heilman's introduction to the Modern Library ed. of Swift's *Gulliver's Travels* (1950), p. xx, n. 1. This note is omitted from the more recent ed. (1969).

Cross-Cultural Considerations

Art, Culture, and the Gospel of Jesus Christ: A Hawaiian Perspective

Ishmael W. Stagner, II

In the Hawaiian language it is difficult to find the equivalent of the English word *culture*. The closest approximation to the word *art* is *hōike* which means "to demonstrate" or "to show." Another closely related term is *no 'eau* which means "skillful," "dexterous," or "creative."[1] For the most part, however, the definition of art and culture in the Western sense remains problematic in Hawaiian, because, to the ancient Hawaiian, it was impossible to separate culture, art, and religion in a complete person. All three were part of a sense of personal direction in life, a guide that came from within the person himself through the exercise of a special power called *hā,* the "breath of life." When Hawaiians met, they interlocked little fingers and rubbed noses; one would then say, "Alo-hā," prolonging the third syllable, *hā.* The recipient of the greeting would inhale upon the exhalation of the *hā* and respond similarly. This was a special greeting, one not used indiscriminately, because the *hā* was the greatest gift the Hawaiian could share. No greater compliment could be paid someone than to greet him with a hearty and sincere *aloha.*[2]

In this respect, then, the worst thing a Hawaiian could be was *hā-ole,* without hā. People of the same spirit were the Hawaiian's *o-hā-na,* family. He expressed his appreciation or *ma-hā-lo.* The word *soul* in Hawaiian is *'uhane,* and to be soulless is to be *'uhane ole.* Alma in his description of the final state of the wicked says that they are "without feeling" or, as the Hawaiian says, *'uhane ole.*

But what has this to do with culture, the arts, and the restored gospel of Jesus Christ? For a Hawaiian who understands his Hawaiian heritage and the truths of the revealed gospel, the answer is "everything." I say this because, having been a Polynesian entertainer for a portion of my life and a member of the Church for much of my life, I can appreciate the interplay between my culture and my religion.[3] However, to verify my perception, I went to other members of the Church who were or are recognized authorities on various aspects of Hawaiian culture. Included in this group are Mary Kawena Pukui,[4] lexicographer, author, composer of more than three hundred songs and chants, and recipient of two honorary doctorates; Edith Kanaka'ole,[5] composer, chanter, author, translator, poet, dancer, and recipient of state, national, and international awards in ancient Hawaiian dance; Alice Namakelua,[6] composer, translator, hula dancer, and slack-key guitar artist whose best-selling album was made when she was eighty-two years old; and Alvin K. Isaacs,[7] a musician whose radio, television, and movie performances spanned more than half a century and whose public appearances with his sons and grandsons are very popular today.[8]

In interviews with these people, a number of common threads or responses emerged concerning the impact of the gospel on Hawaiian culture and art. First, all agreed that the gospel, properly understood and practiced, posed little or no threat to their culture. In a 1977 interview with Sister Pukui, she reminded me that some aspects of Hawaiian culture ought to be forgotten, especially because the gospel offered better alternatives. In her book, *Nānā I Ke Kumu,* she strongly asserts that Christianity answers questions raised rather than answered by the old Hawaiian religion and, even more important, that Christianity helped explain why the Hawaiian was as spiritual as he was prior to the coming of the first missionaries.[9] And for Sister Pukui that was the strength of the Hawaiian. Nothing he did was without cosmological or spiritual import. All of life was a spiritual exercise in which art—singing, dancing, composing, weaving, carving, and painting—served two important functions: It reminded man of his interrelatedness with the universe and the gods, and it demonstrated the godlike behavior men should emulate. Singing, dancing, and performing were intended not only to entertain men but also to instruct them. Thus for a Hawaiian, there is real significance in Doctrine and Covenants 29:34, where the Lord says, "All things unto me are spiritual, and not at any time have I given unto you a law which was temporal." For the Hawaiian, indeed, all things were spiritual.

Second, the gospel uses art, especially music, to develop personal strength. Alice Namakelua's final words to me were, "Thank God for my music, for without it I would have died long ago. Thank God for the Church, because it taught me to enjoy and appreciate the joy and beauty of singing."[10] For a lady of eighty-seven years, partially crippled, and having outlived her husbands and her children, this was quite a testimony. Yet she is the rule rather than the exception, because the history of the Hawaiian people is a history of a basically happy people constantly awash in seas of conflict and turmoil. Certainly a people who could survive almost total extermination must have had spiritual strengths and resources of great magnitude.[11] So what gave the Hawaiians the will to survive? Perhaps the best answer is in the lines of the Hawaiian hymn, "Hawaii Aloha": "Na Ke Akua e mālama mai ia oe.... Na mea ōlino Kamaha'o no lono mai." ("God protects you, ... the holy light from above.")[12]

A third response to the question of the relationship of the gospel to the Hawaiian arts is that the gospel teaches us to want to share our knowledge of the arts and the culture with others, that in doing so we become greatly blessed. Edith Kanaka'ole, in her acceptance speech for her Distinguished Service Award from the BYU-Hawaii Campus, on 23 June 1979, advised, "Don't forget to give of yourself all that you have; that is the only way your gift can come back to you a hundredfold." For her, then, culture was useful and beneficial only when it was shared. Thus, the gospel of Jesus Christ and the life of service it teaches were totally compatible with "Aunty" Edith's Hawaiian background.[13]

Fourth, a very strongly emphasized and constantly recurring theme of all the informants was the gospel's promotion of the family. The Hawaiian word for family is 'ohana, which is derived from two other words, 'oha, meaning the root of the taro plant, and na, the plural article. Thus, a literal translation of 'ohana, is "the roots." In the native Hawaiian society, family was everything. To a very large extent a person's claim to immortality was through his family. Protection, security, identity, and fulfillment came together when one was in a family.[14] Many Hawaiian chants are genealogies, which were carefully preserved and expanded with each new generation. Thus, quite often the family genealogist was also the greatest chanter, poet, or singer in the family. A later trend in Hawaiian culture was the use of the *mele inōa,* the "name song."[15] Dedicated to a person or a person's family as a sign of respect, this type of song constitutes a large portion of the body of Hawaiian music. Thus, the Church's doctrine of the sacredness of families struck and continues to strike a responsive chord in Hawaiian culture.[16]

Fifth, I once asked a famous Hawaiian dancer, the late Iolani Luahine,[17] how she reconciled her LDS church membership with many of the apparent pagan or heathen aspects of her performances. Her answer startled me. When she did those dances, they were, she said, no longer pagan, because the people watching her knew both who she was and what she was. For her, a Christian, the dances became Christian, especially if they were seen and understood in their instructional and entertainment contexts rather than in their original religious ones. She firmly believed that, among other things, her art was meant to cheer people up, to allow both the audience and the dancer to have some fun. For her, then, the gospel principle of tolerance and even encouragement of culture as a means of having fun was extremely important. Certainly for someone like Alvin Kaleiolani Isaacs,[18] who for many years was known nationwide as the Hawaiian Ambassador of Good Cheer, there was no great conflict between what the gospel taught and what his culture taught about fun.

Sixth, in an interview that I had with Sister Pukui in 1977,[19] she stated, "I'm a chronic scribbler." Ever since she was a young girl, she had written things down, either in journal form or for professional publication. When I visited with her in 1979,[20] she showed me her personal journals, many of which go back to the last century. One of the great losses to the Hawaiian community is the Hawaiian language. Few Hawaiians speak the language, and those who do, do not speak the Hawaiian of earlier times. Thus, much that was written and recorded in earlier times is almost totally inaccessible. In this respect it is interesting to note that the 1854 Hawaiian edition of the Book of Mormon stands out as a major document exemplifying the clarity and beauty of the nineteenth-century Hawaiian language.[21] Certainly, if culture helps to give a people an identity, then language, as an aspect of culture, plays a critical role in establishing and defining that identity. The gospel emphasis on preserving cultural records is not lost on the Hawaiians or, for that matter, on any other Polynesian peoples.

Seventh, unlike the severe austerity and conservatism that quite often characterized many of the Calvinist Hawaiian churches, the Mormon church has always been seen as promoting the performance and exhibition of Hawaiian arts and crafts. Many early Mormon missionary journals that mention the gathering of the Saints at conference describe the singing and dancing contests and the festivals that were always part of those conferences.[22] In fact, Brother Alvin Isaacs vividly remembers how his family would prepare for months to go down to Laie at conference time to compete in the musical and oratorical contests.[23] He mentioned that his mother especially looked forward to the opportunity of displaying her quilts, feather leis, and woven mats at conference time. In fact, these festivals and competitions were so important that many non-Mormons came to the conferences as either observers or participants. Thus, a great deal of missionary work was done by the Church through its promotion of these various contests. Moreover, leading singers, musicians, chanters, and composers who were not LDS were invited to participate either as judges or as guest performers. I personally remember going as a youngster to the local elementary school for a celebration of Laie Day, which consisted of *hāku* leimaking, quilt displays, singing, dancing, and instrument playing, all in the framework of a Church gathering. Indeed, the Laie tradition of the Hukilau became famous through a song written by a visitor to a Church gathering.

After the arrival of the early Christian missionaries in 1820, much of the old Hawaiian religion either went underground or disappeared totally. What survived of the old religion after the initial onslaught of Christianity was assimilated into Hawaiian culture as the "new" Hawaiian religion. In form, structure, and nomenclature it was Christian, but much of the spiritual intensity, fervor, and dedication of the members remained basically Hawaiian. However, the metaphysics of the earlier religion, which saw God, nature, and art as aspects of each other, were lost in the argument over whether God and art are compatible. The early missionaries had to make some major judgments about what to save in the culture. The decision to save and codify the language was accompanied by another decision to reconstruct the earlier religion and, in the process, to eliminate or almost totally redesign the hula and other art forms. For a number of years in Hawaii, much of the hula and its metaphysical ties to the Hawaiian universe were taught either secretly or not at all. Thus, Edith Kanaka'ole, whose chants were as much biological, zoological, and botanical as they were cultural, was in every sense of the term a real treasure. For her, the cultural gifts she had as a poet, dancer, and composer reinforced her testimony of the gospel. For her, the message of her Hawaiian culture and the message of the gospel were the same: We must live and love unselfishly, because that's the only way we enlarge our souls. Her favorite saying was, "Ulu a'e Ke welina a ke aloha" ("The growth of love is the essence within the soul"). Many young Hawaiians have a real concern as to whether they can be both all-Hawaiian and all-Christian. They perceive a real dichotomy between the two. But for people such as Edith Kanaka'ole, Mary Kawena Pukui, Alice Namakelua, and Alvin Isaacs there was and is no conflict: They know that art, culture, and the gospel of Jesus Christ teach us to love each other and to give thanks to supreme forces—both outside and within us. If we are honest in this pursuit, nothing more can be asked of us by God, however he is defined, or by our fellowmen. Even more important, having taken instruction from these *kupuna*[24] in what both the culture and the gospel have to offer, we should see, as they do, that there is conflict only when we do not understand and appreciate both. If, indeed, "Aloha ke akua" ("God is Love")—and both Hawaiian culture and the gospel emphasize that—we as a people are and always will be one with our God, our fellowmen, and ourselves. Then we can say in gratitude to all the *kupuna* who have been our *kumu*,[25] "Ina ua like i'ini o ka po'e Hawaii me kou i'ini, e mau ana no ka lahui" ("If we, the Hawaiians, had desires such as yours, we should never perish as a people").

Notes

1. Mary K. Pukui and Samuel Elbert, *Hawaiian Dictionary* (Honolulu: University of Hawaii Press, 1971), pp. 71, 247.

2. This description of the concept of *hā* comes to me from two different sources: Sam Kaai (from Maui) and Paul Elia, (from Molokai). A variant explanation of the word *hā-ole* is that the Hawaiians noticed that rather than exchange hā, the early missionaries shook hands; hence they were without *hā*.

3. My mother, Pansy Kaulaleilehua Akona, was for more than fifty years a respected *kumu hula,* or dance instructor. It was from her and other Hawaiian instructors such as Mary Kawena Pukui that I received much of my Hawaiian training.

4. Dr. Mary Kawena Pukui became a member of the Church through her grandmother, who was one of the first Hawaiians to join the Church. Dr. Pukui, who is eighty-three years old, began her writings on Hawaiian culture

while she was a researcher at the Bishop Museum in Honolulu. She coauthored, along with Dr. Samuel Elbert, the *Hawaiian Dictionary,* which is regarded as the definitive dictionary of the Hawaiian language. She has authored more than a hundred other books, monographs, pamphlets, and documents on Hawaiian language and culture. Her husband, Napoleon Kalolii, was born in Iosepa, the Hawaiian settlement in Utah, and they were married by Judge Abraham Fernandez, who also baptized Queen Liliuokalani, the last Hawaiian monarch.

5. Edith Kanaka'ole was one of my longtime friends. Two days after my last visit with her, she passed away.

6. Alice Namakelua's musical training took a very interesting direction when her singing skills were brought to the attention of the deposed Hawaiian Queen Liliuokalani. For three years the young Alice was personally tutored by the queen in singing, phrasing, interpretation, and composition. She estimates that she has written more than four hundred songs and has supplied Hawaiian lyrics for the songs of other writers. For many years she wrote songs, skits, and plays for the Primary Association, and she was a branch, ward, and stake music director for more than forty years. She and my mother frequently presented hula shows for American servicemen during World War II.

7. Brother Alvin Isaacs's family has been active in the Church since the time of their grandfather, who was one of the first Chinese to be called on an LDS mission in Hawaii. For many years Brother Isaacs played the guitar for band leader Harry Owens, of "Sweet Leilani" fame. He also knew Charles E. King, the writer of many famous Hawaiian songs, and Johnny Noble, who wrote and collected many songs. Interestingly, Brother Isaacs's most famous song, "No Huhu" ("Don't Get Mad") was originally written for a seventies quorum fund-raising program.

8. Missing from this group is John Kamealoha Almeida, who has written more than a thousand compositions during a music career that started in 1915. He is credited with having written the Hawaiian religious song "Kanaka Waiwai," which is among the most popular of all Hawaiian songs. Brother Almeida, who has been blind since birth, has been called for years, "the dean of Hawaiian composers."

9. Mary K. Pukui, E. W. Haertig, and Catherine A. Lee, *Nānā I ke kumu* (Honolulu: Queen Liliuokalani Children's Center, 1972).

10. Alice Namakelua, interview, 9 October 1979.

11. Statisticians estimate that between 1778 and 1878 the native Hawaiian population dropped from 300,000 to fewer than 100,000. See Leonard Lueras, "Hawaiians Making Comeback on Statistical Charts," *Honolulu Advertiser,* 12 March 1977. See also Samuel Kamakau, *Ruling Chiefs of Hawaii* (Honolulu: The Kamehameha Schools Press, 1961), pp. 299–345. Kamakau's original text, written in the 1860s, was in Hawaiian. Not all of it has been translated into English.

12. Samuel H. Elbert and Noelani Mahoe, *Nā Mele o Hawaii Nei* (Honolulu: University of Hawaii Press, 1970), p. 44.

13. Edith Kanaka'ole, Acceptance Speech, 24th Annual Commencement Exercises, Brigham Young University–Hawaii Campus, 23 June 1979, tape recording.

14. Pukui, Haertig, and Lee, *Nānā I ke kumu*, pp. 166–74.

15. Elbert and Mahoe, *Nā Mele o Hawaii Nei*, pp. 3–9.

16. See Alma 43:45, D&C 20:47, D&C 75:28, and D&C 136:11.

17. Iolani Luahine, interview, March 1977. This was one of the last public appearances of Sister Luahine. She died in November 1978 and was mourned throughout the state of Hawaii. Regarded for years as the foremost interpreter of the Hawaiian chant dance forms, she received the Order of Distinction for Cultural Leadership from the state of Hawaii.

18. Alvin Kaleolani Isaacs, interview, 12 October 1979.

19. Mary Kawena Pukui, interview, 6 May 1977.

20. Mary Kawena Pukui, interview, 25 October 1979.

21. The 1854 translation of the Book of Mormon into Hawaiian was the sixth translation of the Book of Mormon into another language. The translation itself is even more remarkable when one considers that the two translators, George Q. Cannon and his Hawaiian partner, Jonathan H. Napela, were dealing with a native language still being codified by Hawaiian linguists and Protestant clergy, after the arrival of that clergy in 1820.

22. An excellent and fuller description can be found in Joseph H. Spurrier, "Sandwich Island Saints" (unpublished manuscript, Brigham Young University–Hawaii Campus, 1979).

23. Laie Day is no longer celebrated. Neither are there any more Church-sponsored hukilaus, both activities having been assumed by either the BYU–Hawaii Campus or the Polynesian Cultural Center. The original hukilau site is now either covered with beach homes or is part of the Malaekahana State Park. About all that remains of the hukilau is the song itself, written by Jack Owens in 1948.

24. The word *kupuna* means "sage" or "wise person." The Hawaiians equated wisdom with age. Thus, in my research I interviewed people whose ages ranged from sixty-five to eighty-seven.

25. The word *kumu* currently refers to a teacher, but originally it meant a foundation, base, or source. I have tried to use *kumu* in its current sense. Among other things, a kumu was responsible for teaching men their relationship to other men by emphasizing similarities rather than differences. It was in this respect that the Hawaiian Mormon *kupuna* probably made their greatest contribution. They used what they knew from the gospel and their culture to emphasize the *hā* of all men.

Divergent Cultures
and Gospel
Brotherhood

Richard G. Oman

The cultural flowering of Zion was heavily dependent on the immigration of European converts. During the latter half of the nineteenth century, thousands of converts gathered to the Zion of the Intermountain West. Many were from the British Isles, Scandinavia, and northwestern Europe. The majority were successfully integrated into the Church, thus enhancing Mormonism. William Ridges, an English convert from Australia, built the Tabernacle organ. Most of the early organists and choir conductors in the Salt Lake Tabernacle were British-born. Karl Maeser, a brilliant educator from Germany, gave shape to Brigham Young University in its early years. Scenes from Mormon history were visually recorded by William Armitage, Alfred Lambourne, C. C. A. Christensen, Dan Weggeland, and many other painters from Great Britain and Scandinavia. Most of the architectural design work on the Salt Lake Temple was done by a young English convert named William Ward. Many of the skilled craftsmen who did the masonry and carpentry on the finest buildings of the territory were also of European descent.

Without such contributions, the remoteness and poverty of early Utah would have precluded the creation of the Church's rich aesthetic heritage. The opportunity to use talents and training also helped the newcomers feel needed and respected, even though their cultures, and sometimes their languages, differed from those of the majority of their fellow Saints. Thus the arts were a common denominator among the Saints and an area in which they could make a unique contribution, raising their own status and that of their countrymen. Bonds of mutual respect were built between American-born and immigrant Saints.

However, the twentieth-century gathering, particularly since World War II, differs in two major ways from that of the nineteenth century. First, members have been encouraged to gather to wards and stakes in their own lands. Second, and of greater significance, the greatest number of converts outside the United States no longer comes from Europe. There are now more members of the Church in Mexico than in all of Europe, and Guatemala has more members of the Church than Norway, Sweden, Denmark, and Finland combined. There are more Saints in the Philippines than in Germany, and almost twice as many in Korea as the Netherlands.[1]

The cultural backgrounds of the new members from the South Pacific, Latin America, Asia, and Africa contrast sharply with the Western European traditions of most "old-time" Mormons; for this modern gathering to succeed, group solidarity must be built on mutual affection and respect. The nineteenth century provides a model of cooperation, but the newcomers were never such cultural strangers, and the Church was never so geographically splintered as today.

Group solidarity begins with cross-cultural understanding, but such understanding is not easily achieved. Too often members and missionaries from the United States and other western countries see only the technological and economic gaps that separate them from fellow Saints in cultures unlike their own.

The continuing use of the arts as a cultural bridge within the Church requires that we recognize and appreciate art forms unlike our own. A brief anecdote illustrates what happens when members are blind to the art of unfamiliar cultures. Several years ago a member of the Church returning to Utah from the Southwest stopped at the mission home on the Navajo Reservation to visit the mission president. "President," he said, "I am so disappointed with these Lamanites. These people are so backward." The mission president asked him what he meant. "Well, they're not gifted. They don't know anything about the arts and crafts, nothing about music."[2] The visitor's preconceptions about art had blinded him to the fact that he was in the middle of one of the great art centers of North America, and that blindness affected his attitude toward the Navajo people. This is a common occurrence when people from one culture first come in contact with people from a vastly different one.

If a person finds no arts in an unfamiliar culture, he has missed them: Virtually every culture produces quality art. To demonstrate this point, let us consider the very cultures that the Church member was criticizing. Painting and sculpture are the traditional European art forms, but not so among the tribes of the Southwest. Among the Navajos, for example, the finest art is produced by weavers and jewelers. Among Pueblos pottery is the most developed art. And among the Hopis pottery, silversmithing, and carving are preeminent.

There is a great opportunity for Latter-day Saints in particular to gain an appreciation of the arts of the Southwest Indians, because among those tribes the leading artists are themselves LDS. For example, there are seven major weaving styles in as many regions among the Navajos. In three of these areas, Shiprock (pictorial style), Southeastern Utah (raised-outline style), and Two Grey Hills, many of the leading weavers are Latter-day Saints. Similarly, many of the best silversmiths are LDS. In fact, Lee Yazzie, a former student at Brigham Young University, is considered by many to be the finest living Navajo silversmith.

Among the Hopis the number of Mormon artists is even greater. Muriel Navasie and Douglas Douma are among the best Kachina carvers. The late Wayne Sekaquaptewa, editor of the Hopi tribal newspaper and president of the Oriabi Branch, made major contributions to the advancement of Hopi silversmithing. Most Hopi potters live in and around Polacca, Arizona (a town named after Thomas Polacca, one of the first Hopi converts to the Church, in the late nineteenth century). Among the descendants of Thomas Polacca are many of the finest potters of the Hopis. The list of contributors to an exhibit of Hopi pottery in virtually any museum in the Southwest looks like the membership list of the Polacca Branch of the Church. Their pottery is in many leading museums and galleries in the United States and Europe and is valued by collectors all over the world.

Pottery is one of the few remaining traditional art forms among the Maricopas. The late Ida Redbird was their leading potter. Her work was exhibited several times at the Heard Museum in Phoenix and published in many books on Southwest Indian pottery.

Bowman Peywa, president of the Zuni Branch, has been making inlay jewelry for more than forty years. Wilbert Hunt was one of the first silversmiths among the Acoma Pueblos. Caroline Browning is one of the few remaining Laguna Pueblo potters. Isabelle Naranjo, a member of the Espanola Ward, is a fine potter and weaver. But the most famous LDS artist among the Pueblos is Terrisita Naranjo. Her pottery has been shown in three different exhibitions at the Smithsonian Institution in Washington, D.C., and is in the permanent collections of many leading museums. Terrisita and Joy Navasie (a Mormon Hopi potter) were honored by President and Mrs. Richard Nixon at a special White House reception for leading Indian artists.

But despite the international reputation of many of these artists, none of their work has been exhibited in Utah museums. We glory in Book of Mormon prophesies of the Lamanites' future but ignore their present accomplishments. Perhaps our traditions get in the way of our efforts to give them the truths of the gospel; we might benefit from stopping to acknowledge their accomplishments. Unless we approach another culture as we would holy ground, we may find ourselves treading on the finest expressions of their most exalted values, works suggesting that God and the muses were there before us.

Sometimes our zeal to help actually has the opposite effect. Several years ago, for example, both Brigham Young University and the University of Utah sent potters to the Hopis to teach them how to use potter's wheels and kilns—as if the finest pottery tradition in North America were not good enough. Fortunately, before they could do any damage, they were persuaded by a local LDS seminary teacher and a young LDS trader to leave.[3]

Understanding materials, techniques, and forms can help us appreciate more fully the art of another culture. To pursue the example of Southwest Indian art, let us consider the Hopi potter. He begins by digging clay out of the side of a hill. Local sources of pottery clay are often guarded family secrets. Materials for making glazes are obtained by boiling parts of local plants and grinding up certain minerals found in the area. This unique combination of materials occurs only in the area of Polacca, Arizona. The pot is then hand formed (using the coil-and-slab method), hand burnished with a smooth stone, painted with homemade glazes, and fired by heaping burning bricks of sheep dung over it. Using a limited number of traditional shapes and motifs, the potter creates an almost endless variety of combinations as intricate as a Bach fugue. Hopi art represents this aesthetic, historical, *and* environmental continuity. To destroy a part of this artistic triad would jeopardize the artistic integrity of the pot.

Consider also the making of a Navajo rug. The weaver begins by shearing the wool from sheep raised by the family. He then cleans and cards the wool. The weavers of the Two Grey Hills area blend different white, black, and brown wools by carding and spinning to make various shades and hues. The spinning is done using a drop spindle, a simple shaft with a round weight on the lower part. The loom consists of two parallel poles, one above the other, between which the wool warp is stretched vertically. Because the loom is vertical instead of horizontal, the weaver can beat down tightly each new weft (the strand woven back and forth), creating an extremely tight weave that contributes to the remarkable durability of a Navajo rug.

The woven section of the rug is rolled slowly onto the bottom pole of the loom. Thus, the extremely complex pattern of the weave (no two are exactly alike) is rolled from view. Even so, and in spite of the fact that the pattern is not written down, the upper half of the finished rug is a mirror image of the lower half. And even though the weaver may spend up to a year and a half on a single rug, she will remember the first section of the weaving. When the rug is completed, there should be perfect symmetry both between the upper and lower halves and between the left and right sides. But beyond that, the tension of the weaving also should be uniform, so that the corners do not curl. And the colors should be uniform in hue and shade. The actual design can be judged on balance and form.

The arts are a significant part of the tribal economy and do much for family solidarity in the Southwest. Douglas Douma literally raised himself out of the gutter of alcoholism and total inactivity in the Church by becoming a Kachina carver. Now he sells his work to collectors all over the United States. In so doing, he has overcome the belittling paternalism of welfare and has found pride and economic independence. The Polacca/Nampeyo family now has fourth-generation potters. Older generations teach younger generations the techniques and styles of their crafts, and the natural by-products are mutual respect and family solidarity. Frequently artists are leading citizens among the Indian people—the equivalents of doctors, lawyers, and scientists in our society.

Among Southwest Indians are examples of artistic excellence that have the potential of serving as bridges of respect and understanding. And now, when the Church is seeking so diligently to increase the brotherhood of man, individual members would do well to gain a greater appreciation of the arts of other cultures and thereby become more a part of the divine effort.

Notes

1. See *Deseret News 1980 Church Almanac.* (Salt Lake City: Deseret News, 1980).

2. William Hartley, "Oral History with Ralph Evans," The James Moyle Oral History Program (Archives of The Church of Jesus Christ of Latter-day Saints, Salt Lake City, Utah, March–June 1973), p. 102.

3. Personal conversation with Bruce McGee, Keams Canyon, Arizona, 3 March 1980.

Artists on the Arts

Thoughts on Art
and Inspiration*

Johan H. Benthin

Because art for me is a process of identifying feelings by means of creative expression in form and color that begins where other means of communication stop, the verbal description of my creative process is extremely difficult. For me the very essence of painting is emotion expressed in visual rather than verbal terms; I want, nonetheless, to try to communicate some of my feelings about why and how I paint.

Every feeling or frustration has a cause, a reason, and that reason has a corresponding color or form. But before I can find that form, I must identify the feeling itself; it must be analyzed and evaluated and only then set down on canvas. As a Latter-day Saint artist, I want to help the viewers find emotional release valves that will help them find and use those hidden emotions and eventually become their master.

Since it is important to me not to limit arbitrarily the reactions of my viewers, I seek to achieve a consistent balance between what I feel is significant in a painting and my desire to invite viewers to become co-creators. Who am I narrowly to limit reactions, to exercise unrighteous aesthetic dominion? I do not like to provide the viewer with the solution to a visual challenge and thereby rigidly circumscribe his reaction. I wrap up a feeling, and it is up to the viewer to determine how much he unwraps it. I do

*I want to express my thanks to Marie Bohler for helping me capture my thoughts and ideas and for assisting in the English version of this essay.

77

not seek, for example, to paint Moses from the outside but rather from the inside. Instead of looking at the man, I try to look at the world from within the man. I try to put into color and form the feelings he might have had, what he saw, dreamed, and realized that he could not have. These feelings are important and need to be captured for others to identify and explore. I want to give others the chance to step back, to reflect on their relationship with the world and with themselves.

I believe that the key to the greatness or effectiveness of an artist is his attitude toward his feeling or inspiration. Where does it come from? How does he prepare to receive it? How does he recognize it when it comes? How can he best use his talent to put this inspiration into a useful form for others? These are questions that, for me, are at the heart of my God-given talent. To receive inspiration I must prepare: Sheer existence is no assurance that artistic inspiration can be received. It requires a great deal of mental preparation. I meditate. I pray. I strive for a humble attitude toward the creative act, which I look upon as a one-way communication with the ever-working creative powers in this world. One cannot be tense or so involved with self that one cannot see, or the inspiration will not get through. When this happens, the artist can neither create nor help his viewers co-create: The artist is unable to perceive his unfulfilled desires, those feelings still available for exploration.

Once I have the proper attitude and can receive inspiration, the process begins. Sometimes it is just one idea, sometimes several, that need exploration and development. The idea builds in intensity within me, until it finally explodes into creation and takes on form. When inspiration has come in this manner, I have not always recognized its source. This insight comes with experience, with time, with analysis, and with much meditation. If the inspiration can be analyzed without ruining its essence, then an understanding of its source can be achieved that, in turn, will result in a deep respect for already existing creations.

What is my motivation for painting? Why do I create? I often feel that I paint to let something within me out, whether it is an idea, a feeling, or a perception; I paint in order to allow the viewer to co-create with me. It is a process of putting a part of myself on canvas, on display for myself and others to examine and analyze. It affords me the opportunity of further developing myself and at the same time of fostering this development in others. I want to help the viewer co-create with me by exploring the painting more with his emotions than with his intellect. Although I try to lead the viewer through the lands of artistic inspiration, he must, so to speak, walk the road alone. I can show him the path, make it clear and inviting or hidden and mysterious, but the decision to walk the path is ultimately his. The roads to artistic insight are exciting roads that, when walked often, become familiar patterns for the viewer. They can become a part of him and through selection can lead to steady growth of character.

Every person has a measure of unfulfilled desires. I am no exception. Although we often cannot define these special longings, they are nonetheless real, moving forces in our lives. My paintings are these feelings in form. When people see my paintings and do not shy away from their own feelings but allow them to emerge, they too come closer to recognizing and making those motivating forces and inner feelings useful. For me, art is emotion in perceptible form, a way of seeing these emotions with some clarity.

People learn by watching others. Children and adolescents learn through experience to know their emotions and the emotions of those around them. A baby learns that by crying he will receive attention. As he grows and becomes more skilled, he learns not only to influence those around him but also to control his own feelings; and as an adult, he often learns to keep these emotions totally within himself. He lets society dictate to a large extent his emotional reactions. By experiencing art, however, he is forced to look at his emotions, to reevaluate himself, and to establish ever more firmly the concept of what he is. Perhaps this is the essence of the artist: He will not be bound by society and has never overcome the need to experience the relationship between what he is and what he can become.

I paint for myself, and I paint for the viewer. I want to speak directly to him, heart to heart. The language of the heart knows neither the limit of tongues nor of styles; it is the shortest distance between two people. Sometimes this means that communication comes in the form of provocation or suggestion. The artist dares look into himself even knowing how frightening it can be. But when he puts on canvas what he finds, he must also assume the responsibility for providing others with this experience but without taking them further than they would go themselves.

The provocation to self-exploration or self-confrontation is dangerous; it can be devastating to awaken people to their subconscious emotions. This experience is a success only when the viewer accepts the challenge and responds.

To be an artist is to bend the will to the demands of honesty. When I paint, the question is always there: Is this what I want to paint, or am I painting to meet the expectations of others? Is this what I want to paint or simply what the gallery says will sell? It is very easy to fall into the trap of corrupting pure art and replacing it with what others expect. I must make a covenant to remain true to my own standards. We all make covenants to use our talents. The choice is simply with whom we make these covenants.

It is possible to produce a piece of art that is exceptionally well done from a technical point of view but that raises important questions. I once painted a picture that technically was excellent. Many an art critic would have enjoyed the painting. The picture had a magnetic quality that drew people to it and made them dwell on it, but it brought to mind thoughts, desires, reactions, and emotional responses other than those I had originally intended. Is the picture a success? In my opinion, no.

As an artist, I have the responsibility to evaluate the worth of each painting. I must ask whether it can touch the emotional chords I wish to touch. Sometimes the evaluation process takes months. For example, if a picture hangs in my studio for six months and still has the drawing power that originally made it interesting to me, then probably it is good. If it is no longer of interest, the picture is not yet good enough and may require more work.

A painter has a certain base from which he works, namely, knowledge and acquired technique. As he paints day after day, he gradually widens his base by developing his technique. Then one day, through inspiration, he creates something significantly better than ever before, something seemingly beyond his level of proficiency. He must then stop and look at this new painting and ask the question, "What makes this picture better than the others?" He must analyze and evaluate the painting and determine what distinguishes it from the earlier work. Analysis, though, is not enough: The painter must also thoroughly assimilate his technical advances in order to reach a larger base from which to work. From this new base he again strives daily. And again one day he receives inspiration to create something beyond his obvious capabilities. This new creation is evaluated and assimilated and again forms an even greater base. The process is never ending.

As a result of my conversion to the Church of Jesus Christ, my artistic development has taken a special course. When I became active in the Church, my testimony grew; and like so many other new converts, I soon realized the staggering amount of time and energy activity requires. But what else could I do? My testimony and my love of the Lord would not allow me to be less than fully active in helping others as I had been helped and in loving others as the Lord loves me. At the same time I was overcome with a sense of loss because I knew that my painting would suffer. How could it not? Being an artist is like any other profession: It takes work, study, and hours of painstaking practice to develop the skill involved. Techniques and styles must be cultivated, but above all, the ability to receive and listen to inspiration must be acquired, and all of this cannot be done overnight. But at the same time, deep within me, I knew, from the day of my baptism on, that the Lord would always come first. He had shown his love and devotion to me, and now it was my chance to show the same to him. As a result of hours of prayer and long earnest talks with the Lord, I was ready to be fully active, to accept all the callings and responsibilities the Lord gave me. I knew I would have few hours in which to paint, but I also knew that the Lord would bless me. As the years passed I began to see how much and in what ways he began to compensate for the lack of time for painting. I cannot say I created a masterpiece every time I sat down, but I learned to use my precious little time well. I learned something else especially valuable during this period: I learned to deal with inspiration.

I had many callings in the Church, which meant times of spiritual growth. I was called as branch president and later as stake president. I loved the Lord and his children so much and wanted to help them the best I could, so I had to listen to him even more. I had to learn to use the gift of discernment and be ever more receptive to inspiration.

During this period I continued to paint when I had the time. The hours were few but were well used. I do not know when I came to realize what was really happening, but as I attended exhibits where my paintings hung, I noticed it. As I tried to put new thoughts or feelings onto canvas, I noticed it. When I talked with other artists about their development, I noticed it. The Lord had blessed me in a way that I had never imagined. I had developed the ability to use inspiration to aesthetic ends. Much of what other artists spend years trying to develop through practice, the Lord had given me through other means. I was more indebted to the Lord than ever before. The sensitive, artistic use of inspiration was the key to painting the way I had always hoped to. Making dreams a reality, capturing emotions that I had thought lost, and assisting others to experience more deeply is impossible without the proper use of inspiration. Developing technique is a matter of sheer practice, but so is getting the inspiration and knowing what to do with it. Helping others to extend their horizons as human beings is what the artist in me demands. It is in striving to reach out to others and in helping them know more about themselves while I am learning more about myself that I find the ultimate justification for all my artistic activities.

Music and
the Spirit:
A Mosaic

Merrill Bradshaw

The Ideal. The temple was finished. The priests had been set apart and trained and had prepared themselves to participate. Solomon had caused the Ark of the Covenant to be brought to the temple and moved into its proper place. When the priests, including the musicians, had come out of the Holy of Holies, all the singers and, players and a hundred trumpeters united their voices and talents in one great sound "to be heard in praising and thanking the Lord; and when they ... praised the Lord ... the house was filled with a cloud, even the house of the Lord." The effect of the music and the cloud was so overpowering that the priests could not even stand to minister, "for the glory of the Lord had filled the house of God." (2 Chron. 5:11-14.)

Is this not very much like what happens to us when we are deeply moved by a great performance of a piece of spiritual music? The Spirit surges in us with such force and intensity that we are captured and held immobile while the gesture races through us, brightening our whole existence. No wonder that those who experience it have tears running down their cheeks and ever after hunger for similar experiences with music. This great event is a model for all spiritual experiences.

Apology. In any discussion of music and its relation to Mormonism, an investigation of the spiritual aspect would seem to be of utmost importance because of both the nature of music and the nature of Mormonism. Today, when so many long-held attitudes and traditions in the Church are changing under the impact of cross-cultural events and expansion, it seems even more important to identify and understand the spiritual side of our musical experiences and to relate them clearly to the purposes of the kingdom and the cultural environments in which it is growing.

Discussion of the spiritual nature of music is at best an uncertain task fraught with all kinds of risks: controversy, inaccuracy, vagueness, provincialism. Some points of view developed over the last quarter-century offer handholds where the going gets tricky; but because trying to put them all together into a continuous narrative seemed to batter some of the ideas a bit, I have decided to make each as compact as possible and to separate them so that they can be considered individually. However, because they form a panoramic view of their subject, they must in the end be viewed together. So, after reading them, step back mentally and look at them as you would a mosaic—without worrying about the size or shape of individual pieces but instead gathering from the whole the outlines of the ideas as they fit together.

Restitution. When Peter addressed the Jews in the temple in Jerusalem a few days after the experience of Pentecost, he talked about a time of "restitution of all things, which God hath spoken by the mouth of all his holy prophets since the world began" (Acts 3:21). That is a great deal of restitution—especially when we consider that there have been prophets about whom we do not even know yet. But we already know enough to realize that at least some of them were not talking about Wasatch Front culture. As the gospel is taken to new lands and the Church takes root in other cultures, the problem appears more and more: How much of the Utah culture must be accepted with the gospel, and how much of the old culture must be abandoned in favor of the new life represented by the Church? The Polynesians have been able to keep the hula and their grass skirts; will the Africans be able to keep their drums and rattles and intricate rhythms? Will the four-part hymn style have to dominate the musical lives of those new Saints who happen to live in India, or will they be able to continue to use the sitar and the tabla to express themselves musically? Will the restitution of all things include an integration of the cultures of all the Saints as they come to the Savior? It is devoutly to be hoped.

Gesture. " 'What is life?' . . . Every work of art answers that question, every painting, every statue, every poem, every scene upon the stage. Music also answers it, indeed, more profoundly than all the rest, for in its language, which is understood with absolute directness, but which is yet untranslatable into that of the reason, *the inner nature of all life and existence expresses itself.*"[1]

In its most fundamental and primitive sense, music is, above all, an art of time—not time as expressed by the mechanical ticking of a clock or the elapsing of days on the calendar, but time as it is measured by the alternations of tension and release experienced within the deepest recesses of human nature. In this sense music is essentially rhythmic. As it unfolds, therefore, we experience music as the embodiment of this inward movement from rest to tension to release: Our ears detect relationships between sounds, sort them into syntactical patterns, relate the patterns to the inner movements of our own spirits, and understand them in terms of those inner movements.

We term these inner movements *gesture,* because they are expressive of our spirits in a very primal, essential way. They measure the flow of intensity of our inner selves. When the connection between the surface of the music and the inward gesture is a healthy and direct one, we have intense, exciting, beautiful experiences with music. When the connection becomes more distant, academic, and cautious, we have dull, difficult, or awkward experiences.

Roles. There are at least three ways in which we relate to music: We may embody its gesture in a group of sounds; we may, by reading the notation and performing the music, bring the gesture to life; or, as we hear the sounds, we may recreate the gesture in our imagination and enjoy its expressiveness. In any of these roles we may be very active in our response to the gesture, or we may be minimally responsive and simply let the sounds flow over us in a sort of tonal bath. Either way we are responding to music, but in the tonal bath we are limiting our participation to an automatic response rather than taking part in an experience that can enrich our lives through conscious understanding and effort.

Ideally, the active listener seeks in a piece of music those relationships that clarify its expressive nature. These he assembles in his mind in a reproduction of the music he hears, adding the conviction of his own emotional energy to the gesture thus embodied. He thus participates fully in the experience first conceived by the composer and then given life by the performer. In practice, however, this process is inhibited or enhanced by a number of factors. For example, the listener who has had very limited experience with music has few patterns established in his experience bank to relate to the gesture being expressed, while the listener who has had many and varied experiences will have many patterns upon which to draw. The listener who has closed his mind to new experiences or whose habitual responses to new experiences are fear, anger, or distrust will not use even those patterns he has established in relating to musical experience, but the listener eagerly seeking to relate to the music will extend himself beyond his normal bounds and be edified beyond his means.

Parallels. I recognize that some opinions I have expressed here are not beyond controversy, but I have found these ideas helpful in understanding some relationships between music and the Spirit. Many of the issues are spiritual issues, and although the ability to participate actively in a musical experience may not have a direct bearing on our salvation, things that inhibit such active participation parallel the problems and attitudes that inhibit participation in any serious activity, religious or not. Thus, closing the mind to the expressive movement of the musical line is not appreciably different from closing the mind to the movement of the Spirit as it tries to direct our daily lives, except that closing the mind to music has less obvious consequence regarding our salvation. The opening of the mind to less wholesome music may parallel the opening of the mind to unwholesome associations in one's other moral decisions.

Responsibility. Mormons, of all people, ought to be sensitive to matters of the Spirit, even in music. And what is our task in this regard? Ponder for a moment the disconcerting fact that the prophecies predict a "full end of all nations" before the day of the Lord. This suggests that the various cultures as we now know them will be obliterated, that the only institution to endure that holocaust will be the kingdom of God. What music will we sing after the Lord comes? What other traditions will endure? Who will give leadership to the cultural life of the kingdom? Is it not clear that the culture of the kingdom of God on earth is that which will endure the coming of the Lord, that which is truth, pure and undefiled? What a responsibility that imparts to those of us who are trying to build the culture of the kingdom! What a tremendous guideline this gives us as we create and preserve music for that day.

Some of us have tended to think that we would be successful if we could just achieve the level of excellence represented by the Eastman School of Music or the Mozarteum or the music department of one of the prestigious universities. That *would* represent a worthy achievement, but it also would fall far short of our true objectives. We are faced with the challenge of doing for the kingdom, and thus for the thousand years of the Millennium, what Athens did for Greece, or the Medicis for Florence, or the Elizabethan Age for England. We will need the cooperation of all the Saints worldwide and all the powers of heaven to help us reach that objective. And we shall achieve it!

The Air Column. I used to walk to school past a picket fence. On cold mornings I noticed that the crunch of the snow would reflect back to me off the brick walls of buildings as a "crunch" but that the picket fence would reflect a tone. As I investigated this, I encountered the concept of resonance. (Every column of air has a natural vibration rate that is a function of its size and shape; whenever there is a disturbance of the air on that frequency, the air column will vibrate in sympathy with it.) The column of air between the pickets selected from the complex sound of the snowy crunch the one frequency that corresponded to its size and shape, then reflected it back.

What a lesson! Are we not all resonators? Do we not all select from the multitude of stimuli that assault our senses those that fit the size and shape of our own spirits? Do we not all echo from our experiences those things most important to us? But our size and shape are not unalterably cast; we can, by spiritual effort, select the things to which we will respond and thus give back to the world what we wish to send. When our spirits are filled with the things of God, we can select and resonate the good and the true even from things that outwardly seem totally evil. This is what makes it possible for us to grow spiritually; fulfillment of our potential through making such choices is the purpose of this life.

Calvin. There are some who distrust the senses, who feel that somehow God would like to divorce us from sensual experience. To them I recommend the following:

> And inasmuch as you do these things with thanksgiving,
> with cheerful hearts and countenances, not with much

laughter, for this is sin, but with a glad heart and a cheerful countenance–

... Inasmuch as ye do this, the fulness of the earth is yours, the beasts of the field and the fowls of the air, and that which climbeth upon the trees and walketh upon the earth;

Yea, and the herb, and the good things which come of the earth, whether for food or for raiment, or for houses, or for barns, or for orchards, or for gardens, or for vineyards;

Yea, all things which come of the earth, in the season thereof, are made for the benefit and the use of man, *both to please the eye and to gladden the heart*;

Yea, for food and for raiment, *for taste and for smell, to strengthen the body and to enliven the soul.*

And it pleaseth God that he hath given all these things unto man. [D&C 59:15-20; italics added]

I am delighted that it pleaseth him.

The Task of the Composer. The task of the composer, then, seems a simple one: He has to conceive the gesture and embody it so that the music expresses precisely what he has sensed to be "right"–good and true. But like all such tasks, it is not as simple to do as it is to say. It is disconcerting to me when people indicate that they think the Lord gives me the notes without effort on my part. This is emphatically not so. In the first place, the Lord never gives me the notes–never! He gives me musical ideas, and I have to find the notes. In the second place, he gives me no ideas unless I am working on a piece, and then usually not until I have been working on it for some time.

The Veil. That process by which a human being can sense the flow of a gesture and embody it in a group of sounds is very mysterious. Some think of it as mechanical, almost like adding a column of figures and getting the correct sum, but to me it seems much less predictable. It is more like getting off an airplane in a strange land and discovering its features, the people who live there, how they live, and so on. It is more like reaching through a veil to feel what is on the other side. When inspiration is involved, the feeling is sure and clear. However, sometimes only part of a work can be discovered in this way; the rest must be worked out by extension from what is revealed. And only when all its parts are brought into a condition consistent with the proper "feel" of the whole thing does the creator know that it is right. It is almost as if the work had a previous existence, on the other side of the veil, and that the creator's task is to grasp that existing form in his subconscious. He must shape and refine it until the outward music reaches the perfection of its preexistent model – its spirit body, if you will. I wonder if this is what the Lord meant when he counseled: "You must study it out in your mind; then you must ask me if it be right" (D&C 9:8). Yet, after all these thoughts, the process remains a mystery.

Advantages. If we are members of the true Church and if God is truly helping us to fulfill his eternal plan, there must be some advantages that we possess to help us in our efforts. I am not speaking of the casually received and promiscuously published "miracles" that so often creep into discussions of this issue of creativity. God loves us too much to do our work for us. Nevertheless, I do see some advantages in the gospel.

First and foremost is a stable spiritual base of operations. A person whose testimony is strong and whose dedication to the kingdom is beyond being shaken by the minor problems of day-to-day living does not have to revise his basic spiritual orientation each time a new truth comes along. Thus he is spared the intellectual and emotional traumas that otherwise might tax his time and concentration. I cannot compose when my spiritual scaffolding is shaky; always I must solve my spiritual problems before composition can be meaningful. The stability of my spiritual base contributes significantly to my ability to compose.

Second, the gospel offers a vision of the possibility of divine help in our task. I do not see this help as a kind of "he-composes-it-and-tells-me-what-to-write" inspiration; rather, it fits into the category of the burning in the bosom that tells me that it is right. Occasionally I do find ideas pouring out almost faster than I can cope with them, but this happens only after a long, intense effort on my part.

Third, the concept of the kingdom in the latter days is terribly exciting and provides motivation for many valiant efforts in the arts. Those of us with temple covenants should find this concept renewed each time we return to those sacred precincts. Being part of the Lord's work, taking his gospel to the world through our efforts, blessing the lives of our fellow human beings as they partake of the art he blesses us to create – these things are ultimately motivating.

Scripture. The creation and interpretation of art are akin to the preaching and hearing of the word of God.

> He that is ... sent forth to preach the word of truth by the Comforter, in the Spirit of truth, doth he preach it by the Spirit of truth or some other way?
> And if it be by some other way it is not of God.
> And again, he that receiveth the word of truth, doth he receive it by the Spirit of truth or some other way?
> If it be some other way it is not of God.
> Therefore, ... he that receiveth the word by the Spirit of truth receiveth it as it is preached by the Spirit of truth.
> Wherefore, he that preacheth and he that receiveth, understand one another, and both are edified and rejoice together. [D&C 50:17–22]

If we enter into musical experiences with the right spirit, we can be edified by anyone's spiritual efforts in music. But it is very easy for one who is not spiritually in tune with either words or music to misunderstand or misinterpret and thus to sin against his neighbor who composes or performs. Since this is as true with stylistic differences in art and music as it is with cultural differences between peoples, it is hardly surprising that some of us do not relate to some works of art, even to those of fellow Church members who felt the Spirit with them in their creation of the works.

Like the Lord's messenger, the artist must leave some things merely suggested rather than explicitly expressed—not to be coy with his audience or to play games with the critics, but to entice the listener beyond the limits of the easily communicated into the realm where things are too precious to be said for fear of crushing them with sledgehammer words or distorting them with the high-pressure demands of grammar. "In art the best of all is too spiritual to be given directly to the senses; it must be born in the imagination of the beholder, although begotten by the work of art."[2] Some things must be only suggested to the beholder so that his imagination can ponder and his spirit resonate to the precious spiritual wonders on the edges of the communicable.

Variety. What kinds of music are needed in the kingdom? Hymns? No argument. Anthems? Well, all right. Children's songs for worship services? Of course. Music for youth dances? Now we are moving onto uncertain ground. Will we need dance music in the Millennium or in the celestial kingdom? What about love songs? What about abstract music that is appreciated for its own beauty? To me it seems obvious that if we really are building the kingdom of God, we must supply *all* the music of a kingdom. And if the kingdom's music is to survive, we had better make sure that it is adequate to cover *all* the needs of the kingdom, not just the Sunday needs. But it also means that we must make sure that the spiritual substance of *all* the music is of a quality worthy of the kingdom. Even—or perhaps especially—entertainment music must embody a spirit compatible with the millennial vision; otherwise, when the time comes, we will have to learn new modes of entertainment. What a splendid challenge!

Cross-Culture. There are as yet not many who can fathom the great wealth of cultural materials that will become accessible to our people as the gospel pushes into new lands. It is true that our western traditions are rich and elaborate and sophisticated and are now enriching the whole world, but it is also true that the great traditions of China, Japan, Indonesia, India, the Muslim countries, and the many cultures of Africa and South America have a great deal to offer us. Many of us have not yet learned to appreciate our own Bach or the more recent manifestations of western art music—let alone the music and culture of our Lamanite brethren. But in the next decades we will have to take increasing notice of the spirit of all the various cultures of the world, for unless we learn to relate to them in very intimate ways we will inhibit the spreading of the gospel by our provincial narrowness. What a glorious thing it will be when all of us on earth are able to come together and sing unto the Lord, our combined cultures all unified and conversant with each other in love and in song.

Mormon Heritage. I would like to say some words about our Mormon heritage in music. It began with Joseph Smith, who not only established the first singing schools in the Church but was also a regular attender of the music classes and a member of choirs. From the dedication of the Kirtland Temple until the present day we have a record of sacrifice and great efforts among the pioneers and the Saints around the world to have good music in their worship and their communities. We have produced a number of excellent hymns, some of them among the greatest ever produced by the Christian tradition. We also have a few not among the better efforts of the tradition but that, at least for the present, are serving very worthwhile purposes in the Church.

Even those Church members who are not lovers of the arts in general have respect for them and often devote a good deal of time and money to them. We have musical institutions on many levels, from junior Primary choruses to the Tabernacle Choir, from roadshows to young artist festivals, from choirs in the wards to graduate programs in one of the most respected university music departments in the United States. It is not to our credit that we do not make the most effective use of these institutions. It is not to our credit that we allow the natural suspicions that business and industrial people have for the arts to intimidate and isolate our artistic people. It is not to our credit that we too often settle for the shallow glitter favored by the media when we could have the bright cloud fill our tabernacles with the presence of the Lord.

Still, the potential for the positive use of all these institutions is here, and we lack only energy, imagination, and persistence from our musicians to bring them to fruition for the glory of the kingdom. Too often we choke back an opportunity to inspire our people and settle for inept responses because we have not understood our potential for edification. Too often we have settled for mere participation at the warm-body level, when with careful planning and effort we might have enticed some to resonate with intense experiences in music and thus to burn with the Spirit. Of course, harried bishops do come to us saying, "All we want is something simple and sweet that won't take much time." But we must answer such requests by saying, "Ah, you want more than that—much more! And we are ready to give it to you because we are going to inspire the Saints with the best we can give!" If a whole generation of our people would learn to respond in that way, think of the inspiring music we would have all the time.

The New Song. Consider how often the scriptures exhort us to sing. I have been wont to think of the exhortations to "sing a new song" (see, for example, Psalms 96, 98, and 149) as a commandment to compose new music; I have never seen a scripture exhorting us to "sing an *old* song." These exhortations may stem from the priests in David's day who would "prophesy with harps, with psalteries, and with cymbals" (1 Chron. 25:1). The improvisatory nature of such speaking and singing as the Spirit moved the performer could be interpreted as a "new song."

But as I have continued to think about it, I have come to believe that when we perform any music with sensitivity we bring its gesture to life as if it were brand new, with all its original vigor and excitement. In this sense we always sing a new song. On the other hand, when we respond as tired, worn-out listeners, *we* are to blame for failing to hear the new song. Gesture in music must always be fresh; otherwise it lacks that vital force that makes it expressive. And when we fail to bring it to life, either as performers or listeners, we fall short of the experience commanded in the psalm: "Sing unto the Lord a new song."

The Bright Cloud. After all these considerations, what is the vision I see emerging to help us prepare for the future? I see the increasing skill of our composers in embodying spiritual gesture, of our performers in vitalizing it, and of our listeners in responding to it. I see all of us becoming more capable of experiencing the Spirit when it is present in a musical performance; thus we will all be more able to sing the new song. I see an increase in the righteousness and spirituality of mankind, developing within us all a deeper penetration of experience so that we may find and share the good, the true, and the beautiful.

I see our Mormon heritage becoming more inclusive of the cultural backgrounds of all our Church members, giving greater unity to mankind. I see this love of fellowmen removing the fences of prejudice and misunderstanding so that we can communicate more effectively with each other and with God. Finally, I see the Spirit penetrating more and more into the various kinds of music in the kingdom, blessing all of us with its joy and peace. When all these things happen, the bright cloud can fill the tabernacle of our spirits with the presence of the Lord. Such transcendent experiences in this life may be only the merest foretaste of what it will be like when we are ready to "enter . . . into the joy of [the] Lord" (Matt. 25:21).

Notes

1. Arthur Schopenhauer, "Art and the Art of Music," from *The World as Will and Idea,* quoted in J. H. Randall, Jr., J. Buchler, and E. U. Shirk, *Readings in Philosophy,* 2d ed., College Outline Series (New York: Barnes & Noble, 1950), pp. 246–47; italics added.

2. Ibid., p. 248.

Excavating Myself*

Herbert Harker

Somewhere a book is waiting to be written – somewhere, deep-buried in the Mormon unconscious, and all we Mormon writers are hard at work digging up the backyards of our past trying to find it.

It isn't easy.

But that's all right, because when it comes to writing, difficulties are at the root of the work. Ross Macdonald told me once that when he has an impossible problem in his story, he sits and gloats for two days. Problems do not impede the story; rather, it is in their resolution that the story is made.

The nature of the problem itself is not always obvious. For example, we may feel that the selection of story material is only a matter of choice, but this is not usually the case for the fiction writer. His material is already inside him, like ore in a mountain. His work is to find, excavate, and refine it. Some have said that among Mormons the job of prospecting for literary gold is especially difficult. I'm sure it is never easy, but I do agree that a "peculiar people" writer does have peculiar problems.

One such difficulty arises from a confusion of loyalties between spiritual obligations and artistic yearnings. I am thinking, for example, of the Mormon precept that my goal is to become a god. It is an awesome thought, truly sublime, yet a thought that

*Reprinted, by permission, from *Dialogue: A Journal of Mormon Thought* 11, no. 2 (1978):56–62.

strikes more terror to my heart than joy. I have little stomach for power. I confess to a hidden wish that somewhere on the back roads of the cosmos there may be a sunny meadow where gods create not new worlds but works of fancy to amuse their fellows. You know the kind of people I mean—minstrels, jesters, story-tellers—so they won't have to send down to the terrestrial king-dom for someone to entertain at the Pioneer Day picnic. I do not mean to be irreverent. I hope it is not blasphemous to think that there may be a heaven for Whitman as well as for Caesar, and that some level of such a heaven may hold a place even for me. (Con-sidering my progress to date, eternity won't be a moment too long to perfect my writing skills, along with the rest of me.)

There are three things, among others, that can be helpful to a writer: a sense of place, a community of which he feels a part, and a tradition, for out of a long past there develops a consensus of the forces that have shaped us.

A Mormon writer should have no trouble with a sense of place. It was bred in him—at his mother's knee he listened to the stories of Zion. As he grew older he struggled with the same land his father did—a land strong, primitive, variable, yet redolent of life-sustaining wealth. And though later he may have moved away, that sense of place is preserved for him in letters from home, family reunions, histories, the speeches he hears, and even the songs he sings—"Oh, ye mountains high. . . ."

When I was a child in Canada, I spent long days in the fields with my father's sheep. The wind that blew on me then still blows—I feel it every time I go back, and hear its moan, like a voice out of my past. It whispers half-forgotten tales of empty plains and of people grown hard and tough as the land itself.

And the power of this land is doubled for us by the manner in which it came to be ours—given us by the Lord, a New Caanan, a land of promise.

In a brief essay on the writer's sense of place, Ross Macdonald concludes,

> We writers never leave the places where our first lasting
> memories begin and have names put to them. Together with
> our culture and our genes, both of which are in some sense
> the outgrowth of place, these places seem to constitute our
> fate. Our whole lives move along their ancient trails; but
> even when we are standing neck-deep in the open graves of
> our past we scan the horizon for new places, new

possibilities. And as the final shovelsfull plop down in our faces we taste in the dirt that chokes our mouths the spores of another promised land.[1]

The Mormon writer's community turns out to be both a blessing and a curse. Like an indulgent mother, it showers him with dramatic possibilities at the same time that it forbids him to use them as he wishes. He is expected to write stories about *good* people. The truth is that the wholly good person engages our admiration, but rarely our understanding.

An aura of mystery colors the typical Mormon world. A boy raised on the streets learns early the harsh realities of life. He has no illusions about angels rescuing him—he knows his fate is in his own hands. But it is different for a child who grows up faithfully saying his prayers. "Will God save me this time, or won't he?" The possibility of divine intervention is always there, and if help comes often enough, on terms satisfactory to the supplicator, then he continues to pray. But he can never be fully certain if his prayers have influenced events. To an adult, it can become an agonizing dilemma.

It is easier to write about such a dilemma if your reader has beliefs similar to your own. He accepts your faith as genuine, and he understands your doubt. But any fiction writer worth his salt craves an audience wider than his own community. If his voice cannot carry across cultural lines or attitudinal borders, he is no more than a pamphleteer, a bugle boy waking his own troops to battle.

What then is the writer's task?

You recall Salinger's little parable near the beginning of "Raise High the Roof Beam, Carpenters"? Po Lo was getting old, and Duke Mu of Chin needed a new man to send for horses. Po Lo assured him that his friend, Chui-fang Kao, the vegetable man, was an excellent judge of horseflesh.

But when Chui-fang Kao returned from his first buying trip with the news that he had bought a dun-colored mare, and the horse turned out to be a coal-black stallion, Duke Mu lost confidence. Po Lo, however, was delighted. "Has he really got as far as that?" he cried. "In making sure of the essential, he forgets the homely details." We are told the horse turned out to be a superlative animal.

One responsibility of the artist is, like Chui-fang Kao, to draw attention to that which is important—to observe the heart, and not the skin only. He must trust or train his eyes to see things beyond their normal range of vision, his senses to detect tremblings before the earth begins to shake. For in a way he may be seen as both a historian and a prophet, recording past events and warning of the future.

Deep in his own heart, since it is the only heart fully open to him, he must search for the truth. Truth is the artist's principal stock in trade—his vision of truth, sometimes the hidden, dark, repressed truth that we, his audience, have been unwilling, or unable to face. He is the spiritual astronaut who gives us a picture of our dark side, which like the dark side of the moon had never been seen before.

It is in his tradition that the Mormon writer is most crippled, not because his past lacks richness, but because it is so brief. His canvas is flat. He must work in two dimensions, as it were. The present, before it can have any depth, must echo resonances from the past. And until these resonances become widely familiar, they are ineffectual; they do not create a response in the reader. If anyone is to produce a significant work that is uniquely Mormon, then it must sound uniquely Mormon echoes that are nevertheless intelligible to the ear of anyone.

More than the conviction of the words and the thought expressed, the real power in writing is the vision it evokes in the mind of the reader. If to him the words have no more than their surface meaning, their effect will be slight, however lofty their thought. But the crudest words, should they summon images of the reader's own, may work a miracle in him—may even drive him to go out and buy your next book.

As William Butler Yeats says,

> All sounds, all colors, all forms, either because of their pre-ordained energies, or because of long association, evoke indefinable, and yet precise emotions. . . . The more various the elements that have flowed into [a work of art's] perfection, the more powerful will be the emotion, the power, the god it calls among us. . . .

> Our towns are copied fragments from our breast;
> And all man's Babylons strive but to impart
> The grandeurs of his Babylonian heart.[2]

The artist attempts to identify the things that move us, and give them expression, not in an overt way—scarcely more directly than does nature herself—gradually bringing us closer to an understanding of our time, our place, our people.

Meaningful symbols are not turned out to order, like kewpie dolls. They're no use, really, until they've been properly aged, like eggs that are such a delicacy in China after they've lain in the ground for a hundred years. A hundred years seems a long time to wait for an egg, but in molding human awareness it is no time at all.

D. H. Lawrence says,

> Many ages of accumulated experience still throb in a
> symbol. And we throb in response. It takes centuries to
> create a really significant symbol: even the symbol of the
> Cross, or of the horseshoe, or the horns. No man can invent
> symbols. He can invent an emblem, made up of images . . .
> but not symbols. Some images, in the course of many
> generations of men, become symbols, embedded in the soul
> and ready to start alive when touched, carried on in the
> human consciousness for centuries.[3]

The symbol of the cross, which Lawrence refers to, has been two thousand years in development, yet we have rejected it because to us it signifies Christ's despair, not his triumph. But if we reject the cross, what shall we put in its place? Where is our Mormon star of David?

William Carlos Williams suggests, and he is surely not alone, that Edgar Allan Poe was the earliest writer with an original American voice.

> He [speaking of Poe] was the first to realize that the hard,
> sardonic, truculent mass of the New World, hot, angry—
> was, in fact, not a thing to paint over, to smear, to destroy—
> for it would not be destroyed, it was too powerful. . . .

> Poe conceived the possibility, the sullen, volcanic
> inevitability of the *place*. He was willing to go down and
> wrestle with its conditions, using every tool France,
> England, Greece could give him—but to use them to
> original purpose. . . .

> His greatness is in that he turned his back and faced inland,
> to originality, with the identical gesture of a Boone.[4]

As Williams makes clear, Poe's method, and indeed his genius, was in stripping his work of the ornaments of the New World, and plunging straight to its heart. There are no Indians in Poe, no mountains, forests, rivers that we recognize. And when he stripped those away, what was left? Terror, isolation and strange, inhuman forces.

But we cannot rest with Poe's vision. We Mormon writers must continue seeking for the original Mormon voice, working with images born, or reborn, to human consciousness only a hundred and fifty years ago. Oh, for a different milieu—some ancient, frothing confusion of a heritage. . . . If only I had been born a Jew I could write novels like Saul Bellow.

Apart from the youth of our images is the problem of their weight. God and angels make heavy freight for the fiction writer.

Eudora Welty reminds us that

> symbols are failing in their purpose when they don't keep to
> proportion in the story. However alive they are, they should
> never call for an emphasis greater than the emotional reality
> they serve, in their moment, to illuminate. One way of
> looking at Moby Dick is that his task as a symbol was so
> big and strenuous that he *had* to be a whale.[5]

How can we produce a work scaled to the proportion of these symbols which we have inherited? God and the devil; divine flesh and blood in a crumb of bread and a cup of wine; baptism by water and by fire; the power alive in men today, by which the worlds are and were created?

Of course the writer will not think of these things consciously as he works. But he is aware of the force they exert, and must strive to give that force purpose and direction. Consciously, he sets his characters in motion—the bishop, the primary teacher, the maverick, the apostate—and then as Matthew records, "Out of the abundance of the heart the mouth speaketh, a good man out of the good treasure of the heart bringeth forth good things; and an evil man out of the evil treasure bringeth forth evil things."[6]

When I first thought about it, it seemed to me that the reason a person writes is to explain—to explain, for example, what it was like to be the grandson of a polygamist, living on a farm in Canada during the depression. I know now that my impulse rises from a deeper source; I write not so much to explain as to understand:

- to understand Joseph; how would it feel for a boy to look up and find himself face to face with the Lord?
- to understand what it was like for Hyrum to kiss his little boy good-bye, and ride away with his brother, knowing he'd never see his son again;
- to understand how men like John D. Lee could become embroiled in the horror at Mountain Meadows;
- to understand my father, aged five, taken from his mother in Salt Lake City to live with "Aunt Lizzie" and the rest of his father's family in Canada;
- and yes, even to understand what it was like to be the grandson of a polygamist, living on a farm in Canada during the depression.

My story is secret, in large measure even from myself. I must discover it and reveal it all together through the point of my pen, a line at a time. And though the enterprise isn't easy, we have no choice but to go forward, with whatever forces of intellect and talent we command, to make our lives, and by extension the lives of our people, real.

Yeats went on to say that "an emotion does not exist, or does not become perceptible and active among us, till it has found its expression, in color or in sound or in form, or in all of these."[7]

In a way, then, we have power, if not to create, at least to more fully realize our world, by giving it expression. We can make our symbols and our language more explicit representations of our thought. It is time for us to get rid of our fear, to forget this inwardness, covering, hiding—to throw our coats open to the wind, unmindful of scars or psychic wounds. If we can do it honestly, the world will not laugh at us. It is not pain that makes people laugh, but sham.

Somewhere, a book is waiting to be written. It is important that it be written, for the promises of the scriptures notwithstanding, our survival as a people may well depend on it. What would we know about the Mulekites, were it not for the Nephite record? Or the ancient Greeks, were it not for Homer? And it isn't enough to put characters on paper, or even engrave them on gold plates—the words we write must have power in themselves to endure.

We have all seen ferny imprints of leaves etched in solid rock which tell a story millions of years old. At his core the writer, or musician, or painter or sculptor longs to match the significance of that prehistoric mudbank—to become indeed what he is sometimes accused of being: an old fossil. As artists, we must try to be sensitive enough to take the imprint of our time, yet strong in the capacity of our work to endure, able to preserve the shape of that imprint long after the world it represents has washed away.

Notes

1. The Writer's Sense of Place," *South Dakota Review* 13 (Autumn, 1975): 83–84.

2. *Literary Symbolism,* ed. Maurice Beebe (San Francisco: Wadsworth Publishing Co., Inc., 1960), pp. 26–29. From "The Symbolism of Poetry" (1900), in *Essays* (New York: Macmillan, 1924), pp. 188–202.

3. *Literary Symbolism,* p. 32. From "the Dragon of the Apocalypse," *Selected Literary Criticism,* ed. Anthony Beal (London: William Heineman, 1955).

4. *In the American Grain* (New York: New Directions, 1956), pp. 225–26.

5. From a talk delivered at the Santa Barbara Writers Conference, June 1976.

6. Matt. 12:34–35.

7. Yeats, in *Literary Symbolism,* p. 27.

Dance Talk

Debra Sowell

The following conversation about dance draws on the expertise and understanding of five seasoned dancers. Jillana, Lisa, and Alexia Hess are sisters deeply committed to ballet. All three began their training with their parents and have also been students at George Balanchine's School of American Ballet in New York City. Jillana has completed her formal training and is pursuing an independent career; Lisa and Alexia are members of the New York Ballet. Derryl Yeager was a principal dancer with Ballet West in Salt Lake City for several years. Since joining the Brigham Young University faculty, he not only has continued dancing but also has demonstrated skill as a choreographer and director. Gary Horton danced with Ballet West and its parent company for twenty years. Following his retirement as a dancer, he was technical director for Ballet West for eight years.

D.S. In the Bible, there are some references to dance that are positive and some that are negative. "Let them praise his name [the Lord's name] in the dance" (Ps. 149:3; cf. Ps. 150:4) is often quoted as a positive example. As a negative example, there is Salome's dancing before Herod or even the children of Israel dancing around the golden calf. Do you think of dance per se as being moral, immoral, or amoral?

L.H. Dance is expression through movement. It's just how you approach it. Personally, I consider it very moral. Movement is a natural thing.

102

D.Y. Yes, it can be used for very degrading types of things, or it can be very uplifting and edifying. It's a tool and can be construed either for good or for bad.

D.S. There are biblical precedents that associate dance with worship, such as the Old Testament prophet David's dancing before the Ark of the Covenant. Nowadays few people think of dance as a means of worship. Do you think dance could be included in our worship, or is there another way your talents could make a contribution in Church services or meetings?

J.H. I think in some ways that dance could be included.

G.H. Is the Church ready, though, for such a move? Dance is very difficult to produce and requires a tremendous commitment of time and energy.

D.Y. I don't know if dance really has a place in regular Church meetings. I tend to doubt it just because not everyone can dance and not everyone can let himself go the way a dancer must.

J.H. Couldn't dance be treated like music?

L.H. We enjoy worship through music and other musical presentations. I don't see why a dance presentation couldn't be included.

D.Y. Something well done and spiritually minded might be appropriate in a fireside or a similar setting in order to uplift people and share the spiritual side of life as only dance can do.

D.S. What is the spiritual side of life that only dance can communicate?

D.Y. It's an awareness of the body. It's freedom of movement. When we came here to earth, we were given our bodies, and our bodies are much more important than many of us realize.

A.H. As dancers we are constantly using our bodies in very complex ways.

L.H. We are, I think, more in tune with our bodies than are people in general. We're aware of the least little thing that goes wrong.

G.H. As a dancer, I became acutely aware of the absolute perfection of the human body. There is a perfection of design and movement that perhaps can be expressed only in dance. This perfection is a function of the absolute and complete control that we as dancers must have over our bodies. This is a seeming paradox, though, because when we are in complete control of our bodies, we experience an incredible kind of freedom.

D.Y. The freedom of flight through the air that absolute control gives has a great deal to do with the spiritual side of life that only dance can adequately express.

D.S. From a technical point of view, there are no steps in ballet that are intrinsically or inherently religious. What is required in order to use ballet to a spiritual end?

G.H. The key is the music. Music has a special emotional appeal and spiritual potential that is only heightened by dance.

D.Y. Music alone is very uplifting, but music translated into dance is even more powerful. The audience not only hears the music but is shown, at least in part, what the music means.

D.S. There are not very many ballets written on biblical themes, but George Balanchine's *Prodigal Son* is one that comes immediately to mind. Is it successful as a ballet?

A.H. I've never had the chance to be in the audience to watch it, but the bits I have seen were wonderful from a technical point of view.

D.S. Do you have any idea of Mr. Balanchine's conception of that ballet? Do you think he was more interested in a story or in putting across the message of forgiveness?

L.H. From what I understand, Mr. Balanchine is a very spiritual, very religious man. I haven't talked to him about his ideas, but I wouldn't be surprised if his major concern was to communicate the idea that is at the heart of the story, the feeling of a father forgiving his son.

D.S. As dancers, do you react to such a ballet more from a technical point of view or more in a spiritual context? Or do you experience such works on both levels?

D.Y. It is difficult for me to distinguish between the purely technical and the purely spiritual. There are some pirouettes in the *Prodigal Son* that I thought were amazing, but at the same time I was able to respond on another level. The way the dancer leaped into the air and beat his thighs together meant something; it wasn't just doing pirouettes to be doing pirouettes. The first time I saw the ballet, I was bored because I was looking for fantastic steps. But the second and third time I sat back and watched it for the feeling it communicated, for what the choreography *said* and not for what it did.

D.S. Let's talk for a moment about prayer. In the Book of Mormon, the Savior was speaking in agricultural terms when he told the Nephites to pray over their crops. To a group of businessmen, he might advise praying about business matters. If he had been speaking to a group of dancers, what might he have said?

L.H. Praying before a performance can be very important. I've asked the Lord to help me with stamina, to help me in taking care of my body.

D.Y. I'm an extreme advocate of prayer, and it's one thing that helped me through six years in a professional company. I pray personally before each performance. Our group at BYU prays as a group before each rehearsal and before each performance. I tell my dancers that we have something no other company in the world has: the Spirit. The Spirit can communicate more than anything else in the world, and if we have the Spirit with us, the audience will be touched.

D.S. One objection some members of the Church have to a dancer's lifestyle is that many hours are spent in tights and leotards, clothing in which the average person might feel embarrassed or immodest. Do you think dancers have fewer difficulties understanding the beauty of the human body than do other people?

L.H. I've had conversations with people about this topic before and find the whole issue very strange. It doesn't seem to bother anyone to see people in bathing suits or in athletic shorts. We're completely covered. Dancers don't give the question a second thought.

G.H. Dance clothing is designed principally to facilitate movement.

A.H. It just enables one to see the perfected body. We think of our bodies as instruments.

D.Y. For me it is a question of believing that to the pure in heart all things are pure. If a person is offended by someone's being in leotards and tights, the source of the offense is within his own mind. Dance is, after all, a contact sport: There's a lot of handling of bodies, but it is not lustful, carnal, or base. The dancers are concentrating on their performance, on their art, on their communication of the Spirit by means of their bodies.

D.S. Another question of life-style has to do with working on Sundays. Performing artists have come up with different ways of handling this issue. How has this worked for you?

A.H. I'd rather not dance on Sundays, but there is absolutely no other way.

J.H. As dancers, we just have no choice.

D.Y. I, luckily, was associated with a company that did not usually rehearse or perform on Sunday. There were times when we traveled, when we were on tour, when we would perform on Sunday, but I never enjoyed those situations.

D.S. Have you ever had the feeling that when you are dancing on Sundays, you are doing something special, you are offering your dance to the Lord? Does dancing in this sense ever become part of your Sabbath observation?

A.H. I feel people should use their talents to glorify the Lord on Sunday or any other day.

D.Y. When I had to dance on Sunday, I felt uncomfortable, but when I finally got into the actual performance, I was fine, because, in essence, I was sharing myself. It's the spirit of dancing; it's a spiritual experience for me.

G.H. I found while I was dancing that perhaps the biggest problem with the life-style that dancing requires simply involved the use of time. To be a successful dancer requires great devotion and the commitment of a great deal of time. I was not always able to be active in all Church programs, even though I considered myself a faithful member of the Church. It was particularly difficult because some members of the Church were not willing to understand that I could be a committed member and not be active in every single program.

D.S. Are there any conflicts of a moral or ethical nature that might prevent a member of the Church from pursuing a career in dance?

G.H. In a general sense, no; but there may be problems with a specific company or in a particular situation. A given company may, for example, want to explore the possibilities of ballet in the nude. This would be a time when a member of the Church might want to consider looking for a position elsewhere.

D.Y. Such situations make me want to move even faster in establishing a company where the LDS dancer can work without the danger of moral compromise.

D.S. What role did your parents play in your decision to become professional dancers?

G.H. My parents were, of course, very supportive from the beginning. My family—my parents and my brothers—have all been very interested and involved in ballet. In many respects, ballet was a family concern.

J.H. Both of our parents are dancers. They coached us; they encouraged us. But we never felt we *had* to dance.

L.H. One thing I think dancing has done is to keep us really close as a family. In some families every child does a different thing. We've been so close because we're all involved with dance and support one another.

D.S. Let's talk for a moment about the unfortunate matter of sexual stereotyping. Some people consider dance to be effeminate and an inappropriate career choice for young men. Do you think that this stereotype is changing, and would you encourage talented Latter-day Saint men to consider a career in dancing?

L.H. I think the attitude is definitely changing. I think the basic problem is the lack of knowledge and understanding. Yes, I'd encourage anyone with talent to consider a career in dance.

D.Y. I certainly agree that it's changing, and changing drastically because, I think, of the advent of some extremely strong male dancers such as Nureyev and Baryshnikov. Ballet seems to go in cycles: There are periods when the male dancer is more prominent, and there are periods when the female dancer is more prominent. In the current phase the male dancer is coming into his own. When I watch a pas de deux, I can't wait for the man's variation, I can't wait to see him jump. It's becoming more acceptable and more respected to be a ballet dancer. The late Paul Hunsaker of the University of Wisconsin did a study of forty-one physical activities and then rated them all in various areas: coordination, balance, flexibility, stamina. Ballet was consistently rated the most difficult and most demanding in all areas.

D.S. Would you recommend dance, then, as a career to a gifted LDS young man? To your son, for example?

D.Y. Yes, under the right conditions.

D.S. Has the Parable of the Talents influenced you in any specific way? Has it influenced your thinking about your talents as a dancer?

L.H. We were always taught in our home that developing our talents is a great road to missionary work. Developing our talents seemed to make an improvement in us and, therefore, led people who saw us to ask about us and our background. We have had the opportunity to talk to people about our lives and the gospel. Such conversations have sometimes been very spiritual and have had an influence on people with whom we work. In fact, one is going to be baptized soon.

D.Y. The Parable of the Talents has had a similar influence on me. It's one of my favorite scriptures. It is particularly interesting to me that at the end of the parable, the Lord takes the one talent away from the servant who had not developed it and gave it to the servant who had developed so many others. That says a lot to me in many ways.

D.S. Derryl, recently you choreographed a ballet entitled *Psalm of Nephi* based on a passage from the Book of Mormon, 2 Nephi 4. Why did you choose this particular passage, and what went into the preparation of the ballet?

D.Y. With this ballet, I wanted to show people what ballet can do in terms of sharing spiritual experiences and to create something that related specifically to the LDS tradition. I picked this particular scriptural passage because it is one of my favorites. As I've talked to many people about it, I've found many who feel the same way; many identify with this particular passage of scripture, with Nephi, who is so distraught at his own weakness and shortcomings. Perhaps the biggest problem that I faced was translating those feelings—that frustration and anguish—into the idiom that I was using, into ballet images.

G.H. I've always felt that it is very difficult for ballet to present doctrine as such. Dance always seems to move toward abstraction in its use of dance images. It thereby overcomes language and has the power of immediate and universal communication.

D.Y. In my handling of the Psalm of Nephi, I didn't want to be too literal. Within the framework of this one passage, I capsulize the entire Book of Mormon. By means of dance images, I emphasize the themes that constantly recur in the Book of Mormon, the promise, for example, that if we heed the commandment, we will prosper.

D.S. With your distillation of the Book of Mormon for this ballet, do you think you have said what you have to say about the Book of Mormon in dance terms, or is there more material that you would like to choreograph?

D.Y. I'm not sure. I've thought about that myself and wondered whether I could touch on anything else in the Book of Mormon without substantial overlap. I keep reading the Book of Mormon. If something strikes me, I'll probably do it. I go by inspiration more than anything else. There might be some other section from the Book of Mormon that could make a ballet unrelated to what I have already done.

D.S. When you say that you go by inspiration more than anything else, what do you mean? Is the process of spiritual inspiration tied to the process of creative, artistic inspiration? When you read, do you immediately come up with dance images?

D.Y. The inspiration comes first in selecting material to choreograph. I get the inspiration to do the subject; then it is up to me to somehow make it work.

D.S. Do you get the inspiration to address a certain topic or theme?

D.Y. Yes. Once I have the basic idea, I use all the knowledge I have to make the idea work within the framework of ballet technique. Many times when I am in rehearsal or choreographing, flash after flash of creative inspiration comes.

D.S. Everything considered—the commitment of time and energy, the sacrifices, the conflicts, but also the rewards and the personal fulfillment—is ballet worth the effort?

A.H. Yes, it's worth everything we have to put into it.

G.H. The personal satisfaction and enrichment that it provides more than justify the cost. It's a great joy to share talent and to help others gain insights and feel emotions that otherwise they might miss.

Facing the Music:
The Challenges Ahead
for Mormon Musicians*

Reid Nibley

Music has always been associated with the Church and with religion, and judging by the words of the Prophet Joseph on the subject and from the things that we understand about the Millennium and the celestial kingdom, music will be an ongoing art. Of course, one of the main functions of music in a religious context is as a help to worship. Music appeals immediately and directly to the emotions; it does not go through the translation centers of the brain, the cerebral parts associated with logical reasoning. For this reason it is extremely important in helping to set the mood for worship and in enhancing and intensifying the feeling of worship. As President Harold B. Lee once stated in general conference, the most effective preaching of the gospel is done when accompanied by appropriate music.[1] Such music is as natural a part of our worship as is speech. We communicate our ideas and, when prompted by the Spirit, our feelings through speech; but we also communicate ideas and feelings through music.

In times to come, music could play an increasingly important part in Church worship. With so many different languages and cultural backgrounds becoming common in the Church, the impact on our music and its use is exciting to contemplate. I think that the Saints everywhere will have to expand themselves to learn to understand and appreciate the musics of other cultures.

In music the Church has been oriented to the hymns derived from an Anglo-Saxon culture; even hymns written by members of

---

*Adapted from an interview given in December 1979.

the Church have come out of that culture. And in a sense, we are imposing that Anglo-Saxon culture on Church members world-wide; through our hymns we teach the gospel to converts. But there is no reason that member musicians from other countries should not create hymns in their particular styles. In fact, such hymns might help make the gospel more meaningful to in-vestigators and members of the Church in other countries. I have heard these feelings voiced by some people: "When are we going to have Japanese hymns from Japanese members expressing their love for the gospel from their own cultural frame of reference?" There is no reason why this should not come to pass, if we can broaden our cultural horizons.

Let me digress for a moment on the question of "Mormon music." People can easily identify our Mormon hymns because of the text; but if we were to take that text away from the music and play it along with some of the works of composers from other religions and then ask someone to pick out the Mormon music, I think that person would be hard put to say, "Oh, yes, this has a particularly Mormon sound." Right now the musical sound in the Church is derivative—it comes out of the culture. We are not writing music in a vacuum, of course, and we are using the musi-cal vocabulary that the majority of our active, established compo-sers know, which is essentially that of nineteenth- and twentieth-century Western music.

Since the Lord first told Emma Smith through the Prophet to make a collection of hymns suitable for the Church, our hymnal has come to include many original as well as adapted pieces re-flecting the Saints' joy in the restored truths. We will always have people writing hymns appropriate to the gospel. A number of General Authorities have suggested that our composers put their efforts into composing hymns and other kinds of music associated with the Restoration. We have not done much in this vein so far, and we might do well to pursue it.

Many of our Mormon composers have said that they are trying to get a feeling of the gospel itself into their music. Whether or not they have succeeded is too early to say. The im-portant thing now is whether or not the music is really honest. I believe that all our composers are earnestly trying to create some-thing unique and beautiful, and out of this effort something is going to happen. I would like to see the day when we have com-posers in every ward and stake, all writing works for the wards and stakes with which they are associated. When we get several thousand composers writing works to be performed in our Church meetings, we are going to get a few masterpieces.

The great commandments the Lord has given his children are to love him first, to love their neighbors as themselves (Matt. 22:38-39), and to acquire knowledge and experience while on this earth (D&C 88:118). Music can help us achieve these goals and obey these commandments and can do so in quite a direct way. And it is important that we use music this way, to combat music so obviously used by the adversary to promote perversion. We need to understand that music can do this kind of thing, that it can elevate. Brigham Young, John Taylor, and others of the modern prophets have spoken about how we can be uplifted by good music. The solution is to learn how to discriminate in our musical taste. We are completely inundated by the music of the world, and through it Satan seems to be doing his best to obliterate any sense of taste from our minds. In the words of one writer, he is sustaining a "vast, overall movement towards the . . . elimination of every kind of human excellence" in order to establish wickedness and a deadness of spirit.[2] Music can heighten our sensitivities, and if we listen to the right music, our sensitivities will increase.

Because music communicates things that cannot be said in discourse, we must develop another level of perception in order to understand what music is saying. Music is related to gesture, to drama, and like them, if it says nothing about life, it has no meaning. It must say something about life. Thus, in the gospel, music can be just as important as words, or perhaps even more important. It is noteworthy that some of the tremendous spiritual experiences recorded in the Book of Mormon are described as being beyond the ability of the tongue to tell; similarly, some moments in music are beyond our power to express verbally. But we sense them; we know what they are. Far from negating the power of such moments, our inability to express them in words seems to give them more validity.

These are the musical moments for which we should strive more and more in our gospel experience. If, for instance, we could play in our worship services the kind of music that would make people stop talking (because of the majesty of the expression) and truly prepare themselves for worship and thus feel the Spirit present, what music that would be! I have known some such moments; I have seen a whole ward choir weep as they sang a piece because they truly felt its power. Such moments can occur in the performance of a simple hymn, too. In fact, one of the most moving experiences I have ever had occurred when a soprano was asked at the last minute to sing at a meeting; she stood up and sang—unaccompanied, because there was no music—Gates's "I Know That My Redeemer Lives." A very simple song, done without accompaniment—but one of my most moving experiences with music, because the Spirit was there.

Such events, of course, come about not only because of the music but also because of its performers. They have to be honest; they have to be open. They need to have the Spirit. The Prophet Joseph said that what we needed most of all was to get the Spirit in our music, that when our composers did get the Spirit, composers from the other side of the veil would join forces with them and would inspire them with music.

The balance between creativity and obedience plays an important role in such endeavors. To me, obedience opens up the doors for creativity; it enhances creativity. Most people think of obedience as restriction, but it is not restriction at all. Rather than being the chain that binds us, obedience is the key that releases us. Actually, disobedience is what binds us, because it locks us in to what we are now and cuts us off from the inspiration of the Spirit and from further progression.

The success of our creative search depends on the framework in which we try to operate. It depends on our goals—on what we are trying to accomplish with our creativity. We might also say that the Lord is restricting us because he asks everybody to be baptized in exactly the same way. "Oh, but that restricts my agency; I want to do it differently," some people say. And so they set up their own ideas concerning the necessity for and mode of baptism. But this destroys all their possibilities. After all, the Lord is still in charge of everything, and he has arranged it in his own way; and if we understand what he has done at all, we know that he has arranged everything for our benefit.

If we go through this door of baptism, our progress on the other side can be unlimited. But the only way to get to the other side of this door is to go through it. So we must be baptized, and exactly the same words are said for everybody. But it is not at all limiting; we cannot even realize until we have arrived on the other side of that door what tremendous possibilities have opened up to us. The same is true of creativity: We must go through certain doors.

The door through which Latter-day Saint artists must pass may seem a particularly narrow one, because the arts seem to be heading in so many directions contrary to the teachings of the gospel. Still, I think that we are equal to the challenge. It is much more difficult to embody convincingly in art the unspeakable beauty of the gospel truths than to embody the lesser values of mankind today; therefore, art that succeeds must by its nature be vigorous and powerful–simple, yet at the same time profound. And by definition such art would be great and lasting–eternal in every sense. The possibilities for progress beyond the door facing us are unlimited indeed.

Notes

1. Quoted in Boyd K. Packer, "Inspiring Music–Worthy Thoughts," *Ensign* (January 1974), p. 25.

2. C. S. Lewis, *The Screwtape Letters,* with *Screwtape Proposes a Toast* (New York: Macmillan, 1959), pp. 164–65.

"The Outer Image
of Inward Things"

Trevor Southey

There have been for some years enthusiastic but often lonely efforts to marry Mormonism and the arts. But with the increasing convergence of the arts and Mormonism, there will (to the extent that we as a people meet the challenge) emerge new art forms that have immeasurable impact on the world at large. I feel this to be almost inevitable.

A large proportion of the significant arts of this century, and particularly in the last decade, has sprung from the despair and vacuum that followed the collapse of the old and established traditions, values, and philosophies. Dominant now is a feeling of gloom, of obsession with the negative and morbid, or–at the other extreme–of frivolity and an obsession with sensual pleasures. Mormonism, representing a direct contrast to this tendency, is, I believe, bound to produce an art form that will be "a light unto the world." I can foresee a time when the eyes of the art world, which are presently focused on the east and west coasts of America and perhaps on some European capitals, will turn to the Mormon community to embrace what might be a new renaissance. The time is ripe. But Mormon artists, and more especially Mormon people, must catch the vision of this potential.

What is the role of the artist in our society? Herbert Read, English critic and writer, defines it rather precisely in his book *Art and Alienation:*

> Art . . . is eternally disturbing, permanently revolutionary. It
> is so because the artist, in the degree of his greatness, always

"New Bloom," by Trevor Southey (etching, 21″ x 14¾″)

confronts the unknown, and what he brings back from that
confrontation is a novelty, a new symbol, a new vision of
life, the outer image of inward things. His importance to
society is not that he voices received opinions, or gives clear
expression to the confused feelings of the masses: that is the
function of the politician, the journalist, the demagogue.
The artist is what the Germans call *ein Ruttler,* an upsetter of
the established order. The greatest enemy of art is the
collective mind, in any of its many manifestations. The
collective mind is like water that always seeks the lowest
level of gravity: the artist struggles out of this morass, to
seek a higher level of individual sensibility and perception.[1]

The Mormon artist who confronts the unknown, is motivated by
and committed to the refreshing and positive spring of Mormon
philosophy, and is subject to the inspiration of the Holy Ghost
should produce a highly unusual "new vision." It is bound to
happen. However, until *we* go into that abyss and bring out this
new truth, it will remain hidden. No others can find it. When the
New Jerusalem rises, I believe there will be a special place for the
artist, as there will be for the builder, architect, musician, and
writer. Such men will be found. But some of us must start this
search now if we as a people are to be prepared.

However, there can be no blanket formula. There can never be
a great Mormon art growing out of directives from Church leaders. Likewise, there can be no blanket formula to achieve individual exaltation. Though all mortals are candidates for celestial
glory, we are all unique. The Church is not (and I quote some
unremembered source) a "celestial sausage machine." If it were,
it would be the tool of the devil. Nor can it be a celestial art
machine.

Celestial art, if it is to exist at all, must spring from the individual as he is motivated by the Holy Ghost. His talent is his, and
no one else can develop it for him. Thus, as I strive to explain my
artistic position in relation to the gospel, I wish to emphasize that
it is mine and that I would never dare prescribe the same for any
of my brethren or sisters. As I have borrowed from others to get
my own fire going, I would be flattered if some day someone were
to borrow from me. But my fire is mine. If another artist's fire is
to be significant, it must be fueled from within–from his soul
and being.

But aside from my own philosophy, "Mormon Art" in general is a relative thing to me. It may be broken down into three types:

1. It is any art form created by a man who professes and strives to live according to the Mormon philosophy.
2. It is any art form that gladdens the heart, lifts the soul, elevates the mind, reveals truth, or in any way broadens horizons. Here the thirteenth Article of Faith may apply.
3. It is any art form that springs from a confrontation of the artist with Mormon genre, history, doctrine, and philosophy.

Where do I stand on these issues? Before I was a Mormon I was deeply concerned about man and his relationships to his environment, his fellows, and his gods. Hence, a few of my past works explore the problems of race relationships, since I was born and raised in Africa. When I joined the Church I made a natural transition into the direction that is now mine. There was no monumental vision. Because of my background I feel the third definition of Mormon art, the direct confrontation, to be the most significant. Actually I find it hard to conceive of a distinctively Mormon art evolving from either of the first two possibilities, but this does not mean that these are not approaches to valid art forms. Still, my excitement lies in the potential of the distinctive quality that can result from a direct confrontation. I feel that we stand on the threshold of a new and exciting adventure. We stand on the brink of the unknown. Certainly I delight in any work that broadens horizons, lifts the soul, and reveals universal truths. But the truths with which I am concerned are very specifically ours: the plan of salvation, the premortal existence, birth, mortality, death, the literal resurrection, eternal marriage, exaltation, damnation—truths restored or revealed through the latter-day prophets.

I take pleasure in the creative process. I am deeply grateful to the heroes of the past who fought against the institution, the establishment. I think particularly of the French realists and impressionists and their battle against the Academy. I am grateful also for the trailblazers of subsequent generations. These have led to a necessary liberation in the world of art. I believe that Mormon art needs to be thoroughly contemporary in its language because Mormonism is a living, vital religion. We must use the past, and the worldly present, as a springboard. We must be leaders, not followers, in developing the contemporary language. I cannot be

"The Moment After," a bronze sculpture commemorating the restoration of the Melchizedek Priesthood, by Trevor Southey (27″ x 27″ x 26″)

bound by any century. I cannot yield my freedom to the whims and arbitrary meanderings of fashion. Likewise, I cannot yield it to any institution—and here I see danger, in anyone's having the Church dictate a stand. Art is a process of continuous growth, and any stipulated stand is outdated and absolute almost before its utterance is complete.

I believe that any vision, creativity, or talent (call it what you will) that I might have has been entrusted to me by the Lord. I am responsible for it. Hence, personal integrity is paramount to me. Because of certain covenants I have made, I have dedicated this faculty to the upbuilding of the kingdom of God.

How can it be used for the kingdom? I see mortality as a time of intense trial, of hardening and softening. All hell conspires to harden the hearts and souls of men so that they will become oblivious to truth and neglect the needs of their fellows. The artist can help in the opposite camp by producing a new "outer vision of inward things," by sensitizing souls, by broadening horizons, and by providing a unique vicarious experience for his fellows. He should be wise-hearted so that he can help to make his fellows tender-hearted. Thus, I must live in such a way that I will be susceptible to the promptings of the Holy Spirit. The peak of my joy is not in the process or the language of my works but in their meaning and in the responses of others to them. I seek to expose my confrontation, searching, and relationship to the truths of the gospel of Jesus Christ, all the time leaving others a certain freedom for creative interpretation. I do not want to preach, or even teach, but only to evoke new thoughts and vision in the hearts of others.

What of the future? There exists right now an alienation between the artist and the people, a rift that must be bridged if there is to be fulfillment. I think that it is largely the fault of the new language of which I speak. The Lord has seen fit to endow the artist with a special and strange facility; it must be that somehow the artist is to benefit the Lord's people. The depths of this new and ever-changing language must be mutually understood. The people must trust the artist and be tolerant of his errors, remembering that he walks a lonely and uncharted path. The artist must be patient with the people, remembering that the strange new language is a little forbidding to them. He must lead them gently. The people must cease to find shelter behind the tried and familiar and become more adventurous in their search. There must be a special kindness and love in this search for truth; otherwise, the result will be a tragic frustration and waste rather than the greatness that is our potential as we strive to marry the arts—the products of special seers or revelators—and Mormonism.

Note

1. Herbert Read, *Art and Alienation* (New York: Horizon Press, 1967), p. 24.

Art and Life

Music:
That Influential Muse

Ruth Hoen

The Lord created this world with an unexampled order. Is this alone, however, the reason why we worship and praise him? Who could ever express in words what moves us when, in amazement and reverence, we observe the fullness of his beauty? How much love speaks to us from the colors and shapes God gave his creation? Who of us has not at least once gazed at the leaves as they dance in the wind? Who has not yet heard the song of the winds? This primeval feeling for motion and sound has inspired men from time immemorial and is expressed in dance and music. When our conduct is in harmony with God's laws and is united with the sense for all that is beautiful, our lives are rich, indeed, and our hearts filled with unspeakable joy. In this manner, we can anticipate heaven.

I was born of God-fearing ancestors. As far back as I can remember, my life has been characterized by prayer and music. I lived with my parents in the home of my grandparents. My earliest memory is of sitting on the floor with a stool in front of me that I pretended was a piano and enthusiastically singing, "do-re-mi-fa-sol-la-ti-do." In the adjoining room, my Aunt Resi gave voice and piano lessons. She was a former coloratura soprano at the court of the archduke of Baden. My favorite place was in front of the imaginary piano, and song and music were for me a glimpse into eternity. When my grandmother and her grown children and their families gathered around the giant Christmas tree on Christmas Eve and sang "O du fröhliche, gnadenbringende

Weihnachtszeit" and "Silent Night," the whole house seemed to ascend to the stars. Everyone there had wonderful voices. It was a sound like that of an organ. I shall never forget those sacred Christmas Eves.

What is it, though, that we call music? What is the source of this phenomenon that so fascinates and inspires man? "I was born of goodly parents," Nephi said. Can that also be said of music, of that influential muse? Is she of divine origin? I believe so with great certainty. We are spiritual children of God; we brought music with us as part of our personal power of expression. Just as our glances express what we are thinking and feeling, just as our bodies are driven by our desires, even so our singing, composing, and music-making reveal our feelings. When our words falter, our expressive powers draw secrets forth from the depths of our souls and give them musical form. Whoever has experienced this in himself will have the keenest desire that this divine spark remain always alive.

If anyone were to take music away from me forever, I would feel myself robbed of a part of my personality. Music is for me the vibration between heaven and earth, indeed, the pulse of everything that lives.

My deepest desire since my childhood has been to play the organ. I cannot explain precisely why the sound of the organ has so enthralled me except to say that the sound of this instrument signified everything that moved my young soul. The financial circumstances during my childhood were so unfavorable, though, that I had to give up my desire to play the organ; even piano lessons could not be continued. One thing remained for me though—my voice. I remember clearly how excited I was when, in second grade, I memorized "Tantum ergo sacramentum." I sang sacred songs like "Christus ist erstanden, halleluja" and "Grosser Gott, wir loben dich" with great joy wherever I happened to be, in church, at home, in the pantry, in the cellar, in the entry—everywhere and at all reasonable (and even unreasonable) times. Thus one Sunday morning at six o'clock I sat on a window bench at an open window and warbled at the top of my lungs "Tantum ergo" throughout the central part of Bruchsal, assured that there were people who enjoyed my singing. But my grandmother was very upset. Running into my room, she asked what in the world had possessed me to create such a spectacle—a "spectacle" she called it—when normal people were still asleep. Now it was my turn to be upset. The song was so beautiful, and certainly it was appropriate for Sunday. And it was such a glorious experience to sing early in the morning! But adults have no sense of such grandiose experiences. My grandmother demanded that I get down from my perch and close the window. Still under the influence of this experience, I climbed back into bed and looked at the pictures in my song book.

There followed a time when we had enough money for food and clothing. The affluence came from a new government, seemingly like manna from heaven. But in reality this "manna" cost a very high price. It was a period when march music played an especially important role in Germany. The nation was programmed for a specific goal: for conquest, for war. Interestingly enough, music was also used to that end: folk dances to establish a love for the homeland, and marches to stimulate romantic sentiments for battle. It was a time of alarm sirens, commandos, uniforms, a time of organized and programmed modes of thought, a time of secret police, of danger, of threats, of hunger for power, and finally of war. The children were unsuspecting. They liked the march music; they enjoyed the sounds and shouted "Heil Hitler!" just like the adults, but in complete naiveté. When they finally realized that they had been deceived, it was too late.

One should not assume that I have anything against marches. I want only to suggest the different ways in which music can be used. The marches rang out belligerently from all the radios. There was no announcement of victory without thrilling introductory music. One could recognize from the blaring fanfares that another airplane had been shot down or another ship sunk. The church organ played only with muted sounds during that period. Nonetheless, my personal life went on.

I studied voice and began singing opera*. I sang and performed as enthusiastically on the "stage of life" as I had from my

---

*Contemporary operas place great emphasis on action, which requires from today's singers a much clearer dramatic art than ever before and a maximum degree of vocal security. It is a very special experience—as in opera—to think oneself into another person and other surroundings, to portray this other person, and to let one's own voice be carried by the orchestra. Opera offers all aspects of representation and vocal expression. Enthusiasm, effort, control, discipline in interpretation, constant practice, control of the voice, and not least of all the contact between the auditorium and the stage make this profession a career of progress and joy. In my experience, sensitivity, the spirit of friendship, and amiability count as the most prominent characteristics of singers in general.

window seat years before. It was a time of hard work but was also pleasant. This mixture of color, song, fantasy, technical trials, and the power of highly individualistic artistic conviction created a very special world for me.

Yet despite my enthusiasm for this profession, I had the feeling that something was missing. I was not completely fulfilled. I felt like a bird that soars but whose flight is always prematurely cut off at the same height. What did I lack? I frequently went to church, but I did not receive any clear answer to my question. At some point, the operatic sequences became repetitious for me, and my intellectual interest was no longer directed toward the stage. In the meantime I had rediscovered my love for sacred music and had sung the soprano solo in many masses. Then, when the time came that I had to dedicate my attention to my two sons, I devoted myself more than ever to my search for absolute truth. I began the search in the middle of life, when I had many questions but no satisfactory answer about the actual meaning and purpose of life. Feeling the burden of my responsibilities, I was uneasy about which was the straight path and whether God really exists.

I received the answer to these questions from the tract *Joseph Smith Tells His Own Story*. This little pamphlet was given to me by two Mormon missionaries who came to my door. Shortly thereafter the two missionaries invited me to a district conference. My first impression there was overwhelming. A very sincere Church song, "O My Father," was sung, but with piano accompaniment. To worship and praise God with piano accompaniment was incomprehensible to me. My heart cried. Something that was holy to me was brought into question. "The Lord Is My Shepherd" was also sung—again with piano accompaniment. I wanted to run away. I asked the two missionaries whether there was any proper organ playing in this church. They told me that at the moment there was no organist available. I was somewhat relieved. Then came an inspiring address by Elder Ezra Taft Benson, and I felt a very definite spirit and a warmth in my heart. I had no more doubt. At the next conference, there was an organist, very much to my satisfaction.*

After my baptism, a very nearly indescribable period of my life began. My particular preference was directed ever more toward

---

*This preference for organ accompaniment to church songs has never left me. The pipe organ conveys to me a spirituality I do not find in the piano. I hear with great pleasure piano concerti of Schumann or Brahms and other composers, but for songs in honor of God, I prefer the organ.

spiritual music. Our Church hymns impressed me very much with the clarity, the love, and the joy that radiates from them. In time the direction of the choir in the branch and in the district was entrusted to me. Thus my musical activity vacillated between opera and music in the Church. Then one day I was assigned to give a lesson on the commandment of keeping the Sabbath day holy. As I prepared for that lesson I was very moved; knowing that the opera performed on Sundays, I recognized a fundamental conflict. As a result of that insight and because I wanted to spend evenings with my sons, who were growing up rapidly, I gave up my stage career. I took a job in the management of the opera, but it was a strange feeling to consign such an important part of my life—singing—to the past.

After I had made this decision, I was left to wonder what shape my life would take now that music no longer played the role it had. The answer to this question came in the completely unexpected calling as the director of the 421-voice Relief Society choir called to perform at the first German-language regional conference in Munich. In Munich, Hamburg, Berlin, Vienna, Salzburg, Zürich, Zollikofen, Stuttgart, and Düsseldorf, the conductors who had been called held choir rehearsals for the conference. Sisters traveled long distances on foot, on the bus, and on the train to take part in choir rehearsals at the central locations. It was not just the music that let us forget the hardships but also the special spirit that emanated from all participants, the spirit that can be felt only where the Lord is central. Ultimately I realized that this feeling was what I had missed during my career on the stage. At the regional conference, there were no professional singers involved, but the spirit and the firm determination to sing praises to the Lord and to bear a clear testimony of the truth transformed these songs into an unforgettable experience, an event the sisters in Germany discuss to this day. Thus I learned that our unqualified commitment coupled with a love of God and a living testimony gives our voices that certain sound that enables us to convey the gospel to the hearts of our audiences. As a result, working with choirs in conjunction with my other Church responsibilities has become my favorite Church activity.

In 1976 a stake was organized in Düsseldorf. The newly called stake president invited me to an interview and informed me of his intention to call me as stake Relief Society president. At the same time he made it clear to me that I would have to give up my calling as choir director. At first I was terrified: There was nothing musical left for me to do. That seemed cruel to me, and it was painful, but I assumed that the Lord must have had his reasons for conferring this new calling and responsibility on me. I accepted the position. At the same time a missionary who had been giving organ concerts as part of his missionary activity was transferred to Cologne. Attending his first recital in Cologne, I sensed that there was something special about these organ sounds that I had never heard before. During the last piece he played, I had the feeling that a heavy burden had been lifted from my heart. And then, approximately five weeks after my calling to the stake position, I was invited to participate with him in future recitals as a soprano soloist. I was surprised and a little bit bewildered because my voice at that time was scarcely in condition, but I agreed.

It is difficult to explain in a few words what a wealth of spiritual impressions and experiences followed. I had feared that music would be taken away from me, never realizing that it would be given back in such richness. I began my vocal conditioning again, but I was plagued by a recurrent cold and had a struggle regaining an adequate technical foundation. In addition, my Relief Society work and my job took my time completely. But to my surprise, this total commitment did not prove confining in a musical or vocal way; in fact, it made me freer and more flexible. The blessing of my stake responsibility had an effect on the subsequent concerts, and the spirit of the concerts in turn gave wings to my work in the stake. When I now consider this unusual form of missionary work, it is clear that it was a kind of miracle. Church doors were opened to us; programs containing the notice that we were missionaries of The Church of Jesus Christ of Latter-day Saints were openly distributed, and we were invited to give further concerts. We had conversations with ministers and with others about the gospel and the Church. We presented copies of the Book of Mormon to ministers and choirmasters and were treated as friends. The higher language of music was able to reach the hearts of men and to bring them to reflection.

We had a most memorable experience in one of the cathedrals near Cologne. When we met Sunday morning at the ward chapel, I was suffering from a cold, was completely hoarse, and could only whisper: It was absolutely impossible for me to sing a single note. But in the blessing on the food at lunch time, we prayed for the health and strength needed to perform this concert. Even so I felt unsure and said that in all probability I would not be able to sing.

Our manager's reply was quiet and clear: "We have prayed, and you will sing. Don't worry!" To this day I am grateful for that instruction. I wanted to sing this important concert and prayed constantly. The concert took place. I stood and sang! I could scarcely believe it; my voice was there.

It sounded clear and firm, even on the high D. This miracle very much strengthened our confidence. At the conclusion of the concert, we and ten members of the audience, including the minister and the choirmaster, had a conversation that lasted several hours.

In the course of this missionary activity, we often heard people ask, "You play the organ and sing? We were not aware of that. You are normal people like us! You are Christians!" Our experience taught us time and time again that music can win the hearts of men in the most loving yet persuasive way.

I recall how, after one concert, the organist assured us with tears in his eyes that, many other concerts notwithstanding, the audience had never had such an experience before. How could we have made it clear to him that we were just as moved by that which had flowed out of our hearts into the music? After another concert, many members of the audience thanked us through the minister for a spiritual experience. Certainly ministers often thought we had come to "steal their flocks" as they called it, but we explained that we had come not to steal but to open the hearts of the people to the nearness of God. On another occasion, a woman came up to me and said, "There is something special about you. What kind of religion do you have? That question interests me very much." As a result, we had several conversations with her. She had excellent connections to other churches, so she arranged several other concerts for us. On another occasion a friend of mine and her colleague attended one of our concerts. She told me later that they had been so impressed that they, deep in thought, had run into a wall across from the church. She inquired several times when there would be other concerts that she could attend, fully aware that she might drive into a wall again.

What a remarkable opportunity music affords us to bring the people of all nations nearer to the truth. Do we understand what a spiritual treasure we have? Let us work with it, not bury it! Let us use our God-given gifts. We should not hide our light under a bushel, but rather put it on a candlestick so that men might see our good works and glorify our Father which is in heaven.

Talents*

Yoshie Akimoto Eldredge

Abraham Lincoln once stated, "All I am or ever hope to be, I owe to my angel mother." In many respects I would like to echo his words. My angel mother was an outstanding musician. As she discovered musical talent in her daughters, she determined we would also be musicians and, specifically, pianists.

From my earliest years, under the direction of my mother, I prepared to become a concert pianist. In numerous interviews in my teens I was asked what my ambitions were, and to these questions I always responded that I wanted to become a great concert pianist. I also recall adding to that ambition the desire to become a mother. As I reflect upon this added objective, it stands out to me as a reflection of woman's natural desire planted in her by her Maker.

By the time I reached my early twenties, I had established myself as a successful concert pianist in Japan and had begun to build a foundation for the same in the United States. I had also become an active member of The Church of Jesus Christ of Latter-day Saints and had adopted values and standards that I knew were critical for my personal growth and happiness. For a Latter-day Saint who is a concert soloist, whether an instrumentalist or a vocalist, there are basic questions and choices that must be dealt with early in one's career. Marriage, by worldly standards and by the

*Reprinted from *Blueprints for Living: Perspectives for Latter-day Saint Women* (Provo, Utah: Brigham Young University, 1980), pp. 116–20.

standards of some of my good friends who are regularly performing on the concert stage around the globe, is not something for which one sacrifices one's career. The thought of rearing children is also unacceptable for those women pursuing such a career. Yet despite the standards of the world among my peers at the Juilliard School and on concert tours, I knew that marriage and motherhood were two of the most important goals in my life and that to be successful in both, sacrifices would have to be made and selflessness exhibited each day.

Now, years later, I look back on decisions I have made along the way, and I am deeply grateful for the teachings of the Church and for my husband and children, who have filled my life with joy and satisfaction. I am also grateful to my husband for his support of my career. We have found in our marriage that no division of work in the home need exist. Instead, each partner strives to fill in the gaps and do what is required, regardless of who did it last or whose duty it traditionally has been. Teamwork in marriage can facilitate the development of a marvelous relationship that allows for the success of both partners. The primary requisite for both the husband and the wife is selflessness. More than any other factor, selflessness facilitates realization of the goal that was ordained of God when he said, referring to all couples married under the authority of God, "They shall be one flesh" (Genesis 2:24).

My husband and I made a decision early in our marriage that I would continue to give concerts as often as possible, even though such a course might be difficult for all concerned. We planned to limit the concerts while the children were young and to increase them as the children grew older and eventually had families of their own. We have since been on enough concert road trips to know we do not want a concert career that entails sixty to one hundred concerts each year around the world. Our objective will be perhaps ten to fifteen concerts per year within the United States, with an occasional return to my homeland for a concert tour.

In recent years, our family has grown in size (three children, ages nine, three, and nine months), and the number of concerts has been reduced to only a few a year. In addition to duties at work and home, my husband was called to serve as a bishop for two and one-half years and as a counselor in a stake presidency for two years, at which time we moved to a new area. He also served as a volunteer for the Boy Scouts of America. All these duties meant he was away from home much of the time. During this time I served as ward Primary president, teacher, choir director, organist, and in other Church positions. I also taught ten or more piano students each week. I found I would go for months without practicing the piano. When a concert invitation would come, often on short notice, I would frantically prepare with much trepidation. Such irregular involvement in music caused me to wonder at times why I had been given the gift of music if I was not to utilize it. I also wondered if the time would come again when I would return to full activity as a pianist.

In the process of this heavy Church involvement, I discovered the true meaning of serving the youth and the elderly, caring for the sick, sacrificing myself for my children, and generally looking beyond myself and seeing the needs of others. I have adopted values and priorities that allow me to place in perspective those choices that I must make in my life. These priorities, in order of importance, are: first, to come to know God the Father and his Son, Jesus Christ, intimately and personally and to learn to obey the will of God; second, to be a loyal and faithful wife to my husband and to do all I can to ensure a happy marriage; third, to be an effective and devoted mother to the children in our home; fourth, to be a laborer in Zion; and fifth, to develop my talents and abilities, including the pursuit of a career as a concert pianist.

Clearly, if my sole objective in life were to become a world-touring concert pianist, my goals would be different than noted (though I am giving more concerts at this time than I have for several years). While I might be criticized for placing the development of God-given talents and gifts fifth on the list, in view of my convictions and experience I know this is right. My devotion to my children as their mother takes precedence over the development of my own talent. My responsibility as the mother in the home is to ensure that my children come to an early understanding of who they are and the purposes of life and have opportunity to learn as much as I can give them prior to their graduation from the university of the home. I am also determined to give my children musical training and other opportunities to develop their skills so that their lives will be blessed with music and with the discipline and work habits associated with musical training. Our children will be mothers, fathers, and leaders of the future, and my firm determination is to prepare those under my charge to succeed.

Notwithstanding these higher priorities and responsibilities outside the field of music, I feel I am progressing as a musician. I recall the words of a music critic in Japan who reviewed one of my concerts in my early teens and commented, "This outstanding young pianist performed the work beautifully, but now needs to experience life and its trauma in depth that the interpretations and depth of understanding projected in the performance will be more equal to the majesty of the composition."

I have learned to appreciate those words of wisdom. Indeed, I feel I have grown immensely as a person and as a musician since those early years, in no small part because of the challenges and trials experienced in my complex life, in which I have tried to make every effort to succeed as a wife, mother, and pianist. As to the trauma noted by the critic, there has been abundant trauma in my life—to the extent that, at times, I have felt I could not continue. But then proddings would come, and after much prayer and inner struggle, I have known it was right to continue striving. While I feel the Lord has allowed tribulations and vicissitudes to occur in my life to expand my soul, I feel he will yet allow me time and opportunity to prepare and display my ability to its fullest to suit his purposes in building his kingdom. In moments of desperation, when I have leaned on him the most, my Heavenly Father has been there to support and to manifest his perfect love for one of his daughters.

Because of all the experiences of my life, my understanding of music and my ability to express it have grown greatly. The expressions of composers, in different moods and colors, come to me as a reality of life, as if such expressions were my own. I become involved in the music more intensely than ever before. The music causes me to weep in its sorrow, exult in its joy, suffer with its desire unfulfilled, dance in its beauty, grieve in its tragedy, weep for its fulfillment of faith and love of God.

There are some developments and growth that take place within us that cannot be rushed, that occur only commensurate with the experiences in life, and that cause us to stretch and struggle and overcome. I am reminded that Joseph Smith, Jr., and other great leaders in history were given tremendous responsibilities to accomplish and yet faced opposition, perilous tribulations, and afflictions throughout their lives. Thus, if it is difficult for me to pursue the development of my talents in my given circumstances, I need but look to the examples of others for inspiration to reach upward. Attaining lofty goals is never easy.

My motivation for the development of my talent is not to gain satisfaction in receiving worldly fame and glory or to compete with others. I always have felt very strongly from my youth that the gift or talent that the Lord placed in me belongs to the Lord. It is not mine. He has loaned it to me, and I am responsible to develop it for his special purpose. I must develop it to the highest level in my power, and I must share its beauty with others around me.

To become a great musician, mother, leader, or a great person in any field, one must work to build all the major facets of one's life. It is similar to planning and constructing a house. If the architect becomes engrossed in the size and beauty of one upstairs room and neglects the ground floor, the entire structure may not only appear distorted, but it may even collapse. This is so even though the upstairs room may be truly magnificent by itself. The ground floor of the individual, his character and integrity, requires continual attention and improvement so that the whole person remains balanced and intact and the special talents and abilities can be properly nurtured and magnified.

To become successful as a human being, one needs to experience the realities of life and develop the capacity to serve others and the strength to rise above the trials placed before him. The happiness and joy of womanhood in my life is a witness to me that my course is right for me, and for that witness I thank my Father in Heaven each day.

Whenever I play, it is my humble expression and testimony, my love and appreciation to the Lord. I am grateful for the stewardship of this gift.

"To Enter Arcanum"

Jon Carroll Lloyd

Much of my time as a physician and surgeon is spent in diagnosing illness, administering remedies, and, finally, evaluating their benefits. It is a methodology that has served me—and, I suppose, my patients—very well. It is, moreover, a methodology that has certain intellectually addictive powers. Thus, I often find myself using it in areas not directly related to medical pursuits and have found that it works in many. Consequently, in approaching the question of the relationship between religion and the arts, I shall begin by diagnosing a cultural illness, continue by suggesting a remedy, and finish by evaluating the benefits of the remedy. As is occasionally true in medicine, the relationship between the symptoms of the illness, its cure, and the indirect benefits of the cure may not be immediately obvious but should be clear at the end.

The cultural ailment that I propose to treat is one that afflicted the 1970s to a degree unparalleled in recent history and one that regrettably threatens to plague the eighties. It derives from the fact that in certain quarters the value of science and technology is overrated and seen grossly out of context, to the detriment of basic humanistic values.

Much of the respect once shown for artists, writers, musicians, actors, and dancers is now given to engineers and scientists. Although the space program, for example, represents an important extension of human understanding, many writers and commentators surely overstated the case in portraying it as the crowning achievement of a decade. The accusation has been made that "the arts are tawdry and in blight; ... literature, painting, the composition of music are shoddy. But Science flourishes as never before. Science is the art of our century." Some may argue persuasively that recent scientific and technological advances in the area of self-understanding, self-improvement, and self-gratification confirm the validity of this assertion. Is it true, though, that science is the art of our century? Can it provide us with the answers, the insights, and the enlightenment traditionally associated with the arts? No doubt science and technology will perform wonders still unimagined, but it does not necessarily follow that their *blessings* will be different from those they have already conferred upon us: speed, power, wealth, and (perhaps) health. Though of value in their appropriate place, these are surely not all that man requires for a rich and fulfilling life. A strictly scientific culture simply cannot furnish such things as aesthetic stimulation and satisfaction, standards of value, and basic spiritual understanding. Consequently, it would seem unfortunate—indeed tragic—to assume that it is to science and technology alone that we must turn for any and all improvements in the human condition. The uncritical adulation of science and the unreflective worship of technology can lead us only to a dark and dreary wasteland.

What, though, is the condition of the arts in the modern world? Are they tawdry and in blight? Are literature, painting, and the composition of music shoddy? It would be tempting to argue that the arts are enjoying a period of healthy growth and development. But Saul Bellow, Nobel laureate in literature, would not agree. On receiving the prize in Stockholm in December 1976, he called on his fellow writers to "return from the periphery." To admonish fellow writers to return from the peripheries to the center—to "the main human enterprise"—is a serious matter. Bellow, moreover, was even more specific in describing the basic problem: "We do not, we writers, represent mankind adequately."[1] His words not only draw the indictment but also identify the suspect. The culprit in this case is the proposition that drove writers and other artists to the peripheries some thirty years ago, the notion that fidelity to life is no longer a criterion for art because life is no longer the criterion of anything: Life has been found out at last; life is absurd.

This fascination with the absurd that is at the heart of Bellow's criticism of many aspects of modern literature has led to many other cultural deformities. Among the most widely read novelists are those who seem to be addicted to producing literature of extreme situations: sexual aberrations, madness, drugs, suicide—the list goes on. Rather than being cherished as a repository of well-articulated insight into the human condition, literature all too frequently is indulged only for its ornamental and entertainment value. And what strange ornaments and bizarre entertainment! How, though, could it be anything else when it is so far from the center of the main human enterprises, indeed, so far from the essence of human reality?

Bellow's concern with reality—his fascination with the central concerns of human existence and his rejection of peripheral aberrations—is by no means new. Aristotle, too, was preoccupied with reality and suggested that the only literature worthy of our attention is literature that deals with the realities of the world around us. Adherence to this principle has allowed the greatest literary achievements to survive through the ages. There seems to be an immediate relationship between what is typically recognized as great literature and the concrete objects of reality. These works get a grip on the objects of daily life; they bring the work of the spirit and the mind into contact with the daily order of things. Homer's account (*Odyssey,* v. 252–61) of the making of Odysseus's raft comes to mind, for in this description there is an immediacy of relationship between artisan and product. When Odysseus builds a raft in order to leave the Isle of Calypso, Homer tells us in the fifth book exactly how it is done: from the type of wood, the length of the planks, and the dimensions of the sinewy hide used to bind the planks, to how to launch the raft. In book eleven (ll. 363–69) Odysseus tells his story to Alkinooes, who answers him by saying that Odysseus has told his story "as a poet would, a man who knows the world." Compared to characters of Homeric or even medieval times, modern man inhabits the physical world like a rapacious stranger in spite—or perhaps because—of his science. He is out of touch with the reality he presumes to control; he is frighteningly alienated from the most fundamental kinds of reality. He paints, for example, better and better about less and less, until he paints almost perfectly about almost nothing. His images on canvas cease being even pale reflections of the central concerns of mankind. Writers, similarly, deal all too frequently with verbal structures that are not anchored in the reality of life but issue from the conjunction of floating abstraction and blatant absurdity. Language is used to mask rather than evoke the reality that is at the heart of all great literature.

The cultural predicament is clear. By overvaluing the civilizing power of science and technology, man runs the risk of creating a world devoid of beauty, value, and meaning. And although the arts have long acted as a tempering force, they now suffer from a certain impotence. Often they are severed from their ancient rootage in the central concerns and fundamental realities of human experience and are drifting aimlessly—indeed absurdly—among the peripheral islands, all the while in danger of being driven onto an inhospitable shore.

The therapeutic task is equally clear. The arts need to reestablish their traditional link with the main human enterprises, the central concerns of lived experience, the realities of material existence. This task is not easy, but neither is it impossible. It leads me, moreover, to the central concern of this meditation: a consideration of the relationship—or, more accurately, one of the myriad possible relationships—between art and religion. What I want to suggest is quite simply that many religious values and insights could be used by sensitive and sensible artists as markers indicating the way back to the center. In offering this suggestion, I do not mean to endorse the facile notion that enduring art is always based on or derived from religious subject matter or that artistic themes and topics should necessarily find religious sanction. I am thinking instead on a much more fundamental and, perhaps, abstract level. Basic religious insights about the nature of reality and man's place in the grand scheme of things, along with other traditional perceptions, could well serve to guide many artists from the periphery back to the center.

What I deem generally true is also valid in a more specific sense for the Mormon artist, for that individual to whom Mormon theology makes a difference. The Mormon artist has a rich supply of fundamental insights awaiting aesthetic elaboration, insights that in the long run could act as an antidote to some of the debilitating aspects of contemporary art and literature. He is surely not alone in pointing the way back to the center, but he has a *Weltanschauung*—a frame, a reference—that will permit him to raise a particularly powerful voice in an especially bleak corner of the cultural wilderness.

Many insights could be elaborated—perhaps even exploited—in this manner, but one particular position well illustrates how many fundamental insights have important aesthetic implications not yet fully realized. If we accept the notion that a basic weakness of some contemporary art ("contemporary" in the broadest sense) derives from the fact that it has lost contact with material reality, then the antidotal value of the position that "there is no such thing as immaterial matter" (D&C 131:7) is most significant. When matter is understood to have existed always, it gains in metaphysical stature and aesthetic importance; when matter is taken to have been organized rather than created *ex nihilo,* its attractiveness as a point of departure for aesthetic creation—indeed aesthetic organization—is enhanced. When all spirit is understood to be matter, what logical or aesthetic sense is there in seeking to overcome matter and become pure spirit? A recognition of the eternality of matter is certainly a compelling impetus for the artist to get a grip on the objects of daily life and to bring the work of the spirit and the mind into productive contact with the daily order of things. Such a theological-aesthetic orientation by no means guarantees the production of masterpieces, but it does assure that the product will have at least a chance of escaping from the periphery and of dealing with the main human enterprises.

The ultimate materiality of matter is certainly not the only theological principle that has significant and fundamental aesthetic implications. The challenge to the Mormon artist wishing to contribute to the art of the center is to uncover the less-than-obvious aesthetic implications of well-known principles and teachings and to be artistically productive in a context consistent with those implications. Such an art may, in the final analysis, prove to be true to the faith in a most important way.

Insofar as ailing art responds to this therapy, throwing off some of its contemporary tawdriness and shoddiness and abandoning its debilitating fascination with the absurd, it will be strengthened and will become more vital and potent in human affairs. On the one hand, art will again be in a position to temper the advances of science and technology: New technological developments will stand in stark relief against the formal beauties of art and the moral values of religion. Advancements will then be seen in a context that invites appreciation and amazement that is not given blindly or uncritically. The accomplishments of painstaking scientific research and technological development can be celebrated while their necessary limitations are acknowledged. On the other hand—and probably more significantly—art that engages the main human enterprises is in a position to enrich and deepen central aspects of religious experience to an incalculable degree by appealing to that part of human nature which is a gift, not an acquisition, to the capacity for delight and wonder, to the innate sense of pity and pain, to the latent feeling of fellowship with all creation. Art understood in this context heightens and deepens experience; it makes religious truths more palpable and concrete. Art does not reveal the truths that save men, either in this world (for that is the province of science) or in the world to come (for that is the sphere of religion). Rather, it makes truths more fully real. It etches deep in the heart the truths that otherwise might remain excessively rational intellectual constructs. Bosch's famous triptych, for example, conveys the concept of evil in a more graphic and compelling way than any abstract theological dogma; a gothic cathedral or many of Mahler's symphonies evoke a more powerful visceral and personal response to the glory and majesty of God than any purely expository description possibly can. The whole concept, the hope, the possibility of eternal life is made infinitely more meaningful by the enrichment and fulfillment that the arts provide.

This evocative and amplifying power must have been at least partially what Ezra Pound had in mind when he concluded his *Cantos* with the statement that his purpose in writing was "to enter Arcanum. To be men not destroyers." Arcanum, the great secret of nature, the powerful remedy that the alchemists sought, is precisely that life-affirming experience of perceiving a broader, more flexible, fuller, more coherent, more comprehensive account of what we human beings are, who we are, and what this life is for.

Note

1. "The Nobel Lecture," *The American Scholar,* vol. 46, no. 3 (Summer 1977): 323.

Art:
A Possibility
for Love

Johann Wondra

As a young man having just returned from his mission, President Spencer W. Kimball saw in the *Graham County Guardian* a picture of Miss Camilla Eyring, "who was returning to be the new home economics teacher at Gila Academy. He had met her once, three years back, at a dance in Snow's barn, but hadn't even danced with her.... 'There's my wife,' he said aloud to himself. 'I am going to marry her.'"[1] After he learned that Camilla lived with her parents in Pima and took the bus to the academy every day, he waited for her one day at the bus stop. "He introduced himself to Miss Eyring, who remembered him.... When the bus came, they sat together in the back seat. For the whole way to Pima, *Spencer talked about Shakespeare and art, certain that was the way to a teacher's heart.*"[2]

Ennobling Art

Works of ennobling art have a great impact on the hearts and lives of men. They enrich life, extend horizons, and allow our hearts to know things that reason cannot comprehend. James E. Talmage teaches,

> The Holy Ghost has frequently operated for good through
> persons that were unbaptized.... Manifestations of the
> power of God, as made plain through the operations of the
> Spirit, are seen in the triumphs of ennobling art, the

143

discoveries of science, and the events of history; with all of which the carnal mind may believe that God takes no direct concern. Not a truth has ever been made the property of humankind except through the power of that great Spirit who exists to do the bidding of the Father and the Son.[3]

Capitalizing on the corruption and evil designs that, in the last days, are present in the hearts of cunning men, Satan uses the power of art to suffocate the concept of salvation and to lead our world to destruction. Ennobling art, though, helps prepare the elect for the message of the gospel and permits us to hope for a Zion where the Saints will live together in a culture of peace, of love, and of beauty, where our lives will become art. I have experienced in my own life the effect of ennobling works of art as it prepared me for the gospel of Jesus Christ. After I came to know the gospel, art assumed for me a much greater meaning, particularly when I considered this prophecy of John Taylor:

You will see the day that Zion will be far ahead of the outside world in everything pertaining to learning of every kind as we are today in regard to religious matters. God expects Zion to become the praise and glory of the whole earth, so that kings hearing of her fame will come and gaze upon her glory.[4]

Four Possibilities for Artistic Impact

Art as a Means of Education. When President Jimmy Carter and Leonid Brezhnev, on the occasion of the signing of the Salt II Treaty, attended the premiere of a new production of Mozart's *Entführung aus dem Serail* at the Vienna State Opera, they were greeted by the applause of the audience: Jimmy Carter very warmly, Leonid Brezhnev more formally. However, when the conductor, Karl Böhm, entered the orchestra pit and picked up the baton to conduct, tumultuous cheers broke out. Mozart and Böhm, the rulers of the heart, were victorious that evening over the rulers of the world.

In 1976, the Vienna Burgtheater, like the United States, celebrated its bicentennial. Joseph II, the founder, was a son of the Enlightenment and saw in the Burgtheater a school for the education of the multilingual of the Hapsburg Empire. His intention was that people of the many nations of the empire, mentally

stemming from different centuries—indeed from different mil-
lennia—and from all the religions of Europe, should be invited by
the drama on the stage to come to terms with one another on the
stage of life in the common language of humanity.

For many great Austrians, the Burgtheater was similarly a
place of education and development. Richard Count Coudenhove-
Kalergi, the founder of the Pan-Europe idea, wrote in his
memoirs,

> We were often sent to the Burgtheater for the performance
> of the classics. The pedagogical effect was excellent. No
> sermon can exercise a similarly strong influence on a young
> mind as a classical drama which is moral in the highest sense
> of the word. It presents the struggle of more highly-bred
> men—of the hero—with fate and with circumstances and
> awakens the desire to die with honor rather than to live
> with vulgarity.[5]

A worldwide repertory that extended from the works of the
Greeks through Shakespeare, the Spaniards, and the French to
German classicism and the present was here formulated. Theater
was always understood as a *Gesamtkunstwerk* in which the arts of
music, drama, painting, literature, architecture, and dance were
united with the purpose of creating examples for life. Each piece
was supposed to contain a moral precept; that which could corrupt the taste of the public was to be avoided. Man's good in-
stincts were cultivated; his base inclinations were not gratified.
How much, moreover, can the educational effect of art be enhanced when we add the related modern media of film and television to theater as recent but important examples of the concept
of the *Gesamtkunstwerk?*

Art as a Diagnosis of Its Time, People, and Society. Through
the work of Arthur Schnitzler we may become acquainted with a
second possible effect of art: its capacity to diagnose its time, to
analyze historical events, to mirror society in a Shakespearean
sense, to warn against those conventions and behavioral norms of
man and of society that herald his fall. Arthur Schnitzler is not
the poet of Viennese society waltzing on the beautiful blue
Danube, of women in low-necked gowns and colorfully uni-
formed officers who have nothing in their heads but trite senti-
mentalities. Schnitzler, rather, presents the dance of death of that

146

society. He holds a mirror up to his age in which the claim of society to limitless enjoyment in all realms of life can be seen. Feeling is eliminated in favor of physical drives. Relationships and affairs—frivolous play with emotions that in Schnitzler most frequently ends in death—assume the place of fidelity and marriage. He awakens sympathy for the people who are ruined by the frivolousness of their age and for those who, in their immature power of love, despair. He was a doctor at the deathbed of this culture. He knew that there was no longer any hope.

Art as a Means of Consolation. The impression of the official guest performance of the Vienna Burgtheater in October 1979 in East Berlin still lingers in my mind. The performances and readings in the Deutsches Theater and the Berliner Ensemble were a unique success for us. The audience, which was absolutely sated with the narrowness of Marxist ideology and the corruption of the functionaries, enthusiastically applauded Austrian literature: Grillparzer, Raimund, Nestroy, Schnitzler, Hofmannsthal, Kraus, Musil, Molnar, Wildgans, Polgar, Horvath, Canetti, Handke, and others, all of whom know nothing about ideologies but know a great deal about mankind, about his desires, about his frustrations, but also about his hopes.

In totalitarian states—like the Danube monarchy at the time of Metternich, the Nazi domination, and the Communist dictatorships—art frequently has the function of being both a consolation and the last treasured refuge of freedom. One example will illustrate the point. At the Deutsches Theater in Berlin during World War II, a new production of Schiller's *Don Carlos* was presented. Joseph Goebbels, the Nazi minister for education and propaganda, was in the official loge. The play progressed to the dialogue between King Philip II of Spain, an absolute ruler and dictator who brutally suppressed the struggle for independence of the Netherlands, and Marquis Posa, Schiller's representative of an enlightened ruler who respects the fundamental rights of men. At the end of Posa's masterful speech about the horrors that he encountered in Flanders and Brabant, he addresses his appeal to Philip: "Sire, allow freedom of thought!" At this point a tumult of applause, stamping, shouting, and chanting broke out in the auditorium. The audience identified with Marquis Posa's appeal. Finally, after fifteen minutes of this uproar, the lights in the auditorium were suddenly turned on, and it was immediately quiet. The play continued, and King Philip II answered, "Strange fanatic." Joseph Goebbels arose in his loge and applauded. He applauded alone.

Art as a Means of Praising the Lord. George Frederick Handel, a recognized and much-celebrated musician, composer, and opera director, collapsed at the age of fifty-two from a stroke that left his right side, in the opinion of his doctors, permanently paralyzed. But Handel's will, the fundamental power of his being, had not been affected by the crippling stroke. He had himself taken to the hot baths at Aachen. Although the doctors warned him that staying in the baths longer than three hours at a time would kill him, he remained for nine hours a day, and along with his will, his strength grew. After a week he could drag himself around; after the second week he could move his arms. On the last day of his recuperation, completely the master of his body, Handel went into a church and seated himself at the organ. He could play again. He could again write operas and oratorios, including *Saul* and *Israel in Egypt.*

The times, though, were against him. The death of the queen interrupted performances, and the Spanish war emptied the theaters. Debts accumulated, and gradually, in despair, Handel lost his courage. His creative stream dried up. In desperation, he threw himself on his bed. "If only sleep would come, to forget, to be blotted out, to cease to be." But something drove him to open a letter from Jennens, his librettist. There was a new text: the *Messiah.* Already the first words, "Comfort ye," penetrated to his heart. It seemed to him that the Lord himself had said to him, "Comfort ye." He had scarcely read the words, scarcely felt them, when he heard them as music. He continued to read: "Thus saith the Lord. . . . And He shall purify." Indeed, this had happened to him: The darkness had been suddenly swept out of his heart, and triumphant light had broken forth. He read further: "O thou that tellest good tidings to Zion," "He shall feed his flock," "His yoke is easy." "Surely He hath borne our griefs," "And with His stripes we are healed." "All they that see Him, laugh Him to scorn," "He looked for some to have pity on Him, but there was no man, neither found He any to comfort Him," "He trusted in God that He would deliver Him." "But Thou didst not leave His soul in hell."

And then he read, *"The Lord gave the Word."* Surely the words came from him, the music came from him, the grace came from him. And they must be returned to him, to honor him, to praise him, to glorify him. "Halleluja! Halleluja!" All the voices of mankind must be united in a great chorus to sing his praise; they must rise and fall together and harmonize with the sweet sounds of the strings and the stirring fanfares of the brass; they must fuse with the joyous exultations of the organ. "Halleluja! Halleluja! Halleluja!": Out of this word an anthem had to be created that would extend from this earth to the throne of God.

"I know that my Redeemer liveth." Surely he lives. He spoke to Handel in this hour of need. Handel did not leave his room for three weeks. Then the work was all but finished, and only one word was still lacking, the last word of the work: "Amen." But out of this word—from these two syllables—Handel built a musical ladder that reached into heaven, that reached the Lord who had saved him. As the enthusiastic applause of the audience filled the hall after the first performance of the *Messiah,* in Dublin, Handel slipped away to prayerfully thank Him who had given him this work. Handel frequently performed the *Messiah,* but he never accepted payment for it. "I am in the debt of another. It should always belong to the sick and imprisoned. I myself was sick and healed by it; I was a prisoner, and it freed me."[6]

Mormonism and the Arts

President Spencer W. Kimball has made a very challenging observation: "In the field of both composition and performance, why cannot someone write a greater oratorio than Handel's *Messiah?* The best has not yet been composed nor produced."[7] It is not my intention to counsel the Church, but within my own sphere of activity, there are several things that I can do to promote the realization of the prophet's goal.

Before I heard of the gospel of Jesus Christ, I recognized that the world desperately needed a message of salvation and that it could best be presented in theatric and cinematic means as a *Gesamtkunstwerk.* I studied theatric and cinematic arts at the University of Vienna and joined the Vienna Burgtheater. And upon hearing the gospel, I discovered that its message is precisely what the world so desperately needs.

The gospel brought peace to my heart. I received the blessing of a family of four children and considered changing my profession in order to enjoy a more comfortable occupation. Elder Eldred G. Smith, however, gave me some advice that does not apply to me alone because it is of general validity. He advised me not to change my profession and said that precisely in the areas of cultural and political life, indeed in those areas where in our time negative powers are seeking to exercise especially strong influences, members of the Church are needed in order to control the adversary, to keep him within limits, and to exert through righteous happiness an ever-increasing influence for good. I recognized that we, self-satisfied though we may be in the enjoyment of the blessings of the gospel, must not vitiate our efforts in the final struggle. There is no goodness in the world that could not be improved by faithful, prepared members of the Church; there is similarly no evil that could not be countered or at least tempered by believing, skilled members.

As a father I can create an appropriate spiritual climate in our family so that the children will be armed against cultural barbarism and so that artistic talents will be discovered and developed early. Periodically I spend a day with each of our children. At the end of one such day, I took our daughter, Ulrike, to the concert hall of the Vienna Philharmonic where Karl Böhm was conducting works of Mozart, Strauss, and Brahms. Ulrike was enthusiastic, the music moved her, the immediate presence of the orchestra fascinated her. Her eyes beamed. She applauded intensely. Afterward we went to the Imperial Cafe to eat a special Viennese crêpe with ice cream, which itself is also a work of art. I told her about the lives of Mozart and Karl Böhm and endeavored to bring her nearer to the world of beauty that is so richly represented in Vienna.

Evil in its raucous, impudent, and foul forms penetrates so strongly into the consciousness of our precious young people that they scarcely have freedom of choice. We cannot isolate our young people from the influences of this world, but we can teach them to differentiate so that they can avoid everything that is unclean, unspiritual, and ugly. How important it is, therefore, to acquaint our children early with the beauties of works of art. How important it is that a family, along with its supply of the necessities of life, have a supply of the beauties of life stored up or at least accessible to them: pictures, books, records, tapes, films, and the like. And how important it is to make use of them in family home evenings and on other occasions.

Great artistic gifts often manifest themselves in early years. For example, Wolfgang Amadeus Mozart, encouraged by his father, wrote his first composition, a minuet for piano, at five years of age; at seven he gave concerts in many cities and countries while on a strenuous European tour with his family and wrote his first sonata for violin and piano. At eight he composed his first symphony; in the following years he composed sonatas, string quartets, piano and violin concertos, serenades, masques, songs, and masses; and at fourteen he wrote his first opera.

A ward or branch, a stake, a district, a mission, or a region can create challenges for the application, recognition, and development of artistic gifts. What an abundance of often remarkably good sketches, dances, songs, and roadshows are created in the course of time by a single ward or branch. Should not the best examples be collected as specimens of Mormon folk art? No nation on earth is as creatively talented as the Latter-day Saints. Have not the greatest spirits been reserved for this dispensation? Should not Mormon folk art along with classical works of ennobling art be collected and stored up as a "Welfare Plan of Beauty" so that the Latter-day Saints can be in cultural matters independent of all other creatures beneath heaven? We live today in a period in which we can scarcely expect that any new works of art will be in harmony which the Spirit of the Lord, unless the Latter-day Saints themselves produce or inspire them.

If one of my children, or another young Latter-day Saint, were talented enough to produce works of art, I would give him five challenges to take along on his difficult path.

First, make the decision to do it. The gospel is the glad message needed for a happy life. Members of the Church, therefore, have few tensions that erupt as artistic expressions. This fact can easily lead to self-satisfaction and self-sufficiency. We know the laws required to live healthy and happy lives and enjoy these blessings, but all too often we are blind to the needs of the elect of God who would love the gospel as we do but do not know the gospel. Let it be your free decision to accomplish the very most for the world and the Lord. Let it be your free decision to make the necessary sacrifices and to bear the required grief: A pearl can grow only in a wounded oyster.

Second, have the fortitude not to compromise yourself vis-à-vis the world. Evil uses art as a means of destroying men—in free democratic countries as a means of destroying morality and in authoritarian states as a tool for propaganda and force. Mao Tsetung discussed culture as an arena for political struggle; Lenin used culture as a tool for changing the world. Nazism had the characteristics of a mighty festival, and under the influence of

Hitler and Goebbels 1,150 films were made. One could easily infer the future course of affairs from them: the persecution of the Jews and the justification of euthanasia. The more authoritarian the political power, the more fiercely it uses culture as a tool. This is possible only because a sufficient number of artists—authors, painters, sculptors, film directors, and the like—rush, or at least are willing, to produce the desired artifact for the ruling power: They compromise themselves vis-à-vis the world.

The Latter-day Saints have never had a greater opportunity to have their work—when it achieves formal perfection—appreciatively accepted. One frequently hears that the world has become so corrupt that honorable men cannot prevail. In purely human terms, this may be the case: In comparison with the ambitious and reckless hustler who compromises himself and aligns himself with all kinds of perverted men to achieve his egotistical goals, we appear to be at a disadvantage. But when we learn to accept the Lord as a partner and to stand valiantly by our principles, he will fight our battles and prepare us a table in the face of our enemies.

Third, strive for perfection. President Kimball has given good advice for the development of talents:

> Members of the Church should be peers or superiors to any others in natural ability, extended training, plus the Holy Spirit which should bring them light and truth. With hundreds of "men of God" and their associates so blessed, we have the base for an increasingly efficient and worthy corps of talent. . . . If we strive for perfection—the best and greatest—and are never satisfied with mediocrity, we can excel.[8]

Goethe admiringly said of the deceased Schiller that he did not touch anything base that he did not ennoble, that every week he was a different and more perfect man, that nothing confined him, nothing weighed down the flight of his thoughts.

Fourth, bless the lives of others with beauty. The perfection of a work of art is its beauty. Eleanore Duse shattered all established forms in order to create a unique and tangible embodiment of that which we call beauty. It is reported that her acting evoked feelings that had never been experienced before, feelings that were scarcely thought possible. In "Letters on the Aesthetic Education of Man," Schiller also expressed his fascination for perfect beauty in noting that beauty alone blesses all the world and that every

152

creature forgets its limitations as long as it experiences the magic of beauty.

Finally, seek the love of God. The key by which to judge whether a work of art is inspired by God or by evil is clear and unmistakable: "Every thing which inviteth to do good, and to persuade to believe in Christ, is sent forth by the power and gift of Christ; wherefore ye may know with a perfect knowledge it is of God" (Moroni 7:16). Art that is from God will praise the Lord and his creations, awaken love and sympathy for neighbors, and never injure the dignity of man. Art is therefore *a possibility for love:* "Thou shalt love the Lord thy God with all thy heart, and with all thy soul, and with all thy strength, and with all thy mind, and thy neighbor as thyself" (Luke 10:27). Divinely inspired art will express a love of God in that it praises the Lord, his creation, and his work on earth. It will promote love of neighbors in that it teaches Christian virtues in daily life. Whoever masterfully controls artistic forms and patterns and has the most love will bring forth the greatest works of art. By means of love, we are one with the Creator and can create as he did. This love is a gift of God that he gives freely to those who keep his commandments and ask for this gift.

> O LORD, my LORD,
> My deliverer, my redeemer, my savior.
> Thou shield of my faith
> Thou rock of my salvation,
> Thou comfort in my affliction,
> Thou alone God of my devotion and my songs of praise and glory.
>
> Oh, it is wonderful to taste of Thy love!
> Give me, O LORD, the love that is in Thee,
> So that it may be in me,
> And I, thus, may be in Thee,
> So that the times may be accomplished
> When all the world will praise Thee eternally.

Notes

1. Edward L. Kimball and Andrew E. Kimball, Jr., *Spencer W. Kimball: Twelfth President of The Church of Jesus Christ of Latter-day Saints* (Salt Lake City: Bookcraft, 1977), p. 83.

2. Ibid., p. 84.

3. *The Articles of Faith,* 12th ed. (Salt Lake City: The Church of Jesus Christ of Latter-day Saints, 1924), pp. 164–65.

4. Sermon delivered 20 September 1857; see *The Messenger,* July 1953.

5. Cited by Fred Hennings, *Heimat Burgtheater 1* (Vienna: n.p., 1972), p. 19.

6. See Stefan Zweig, *The Tide of Fortune: Twelve Historical Miniatures,* trans. Eden and Cedar Paul (London: Cassel and Co., 1940), pp. 100–126.

7. Spencer W. Kimball, "The Gospel Vision of the Arts," *Ensign,* July 1977, p. 3.

8. Ibid.

List of
Contributors

Johan H. Benthin, whose "Collage" appears on the front cover of this volume, is the son and grandson of painters. Born in Copenhagen, Denmark, he characterizes himself as "an individual needing vigorous development through friends and family to be able to create effectively." He has traveled extensively in the Americas, Africa, and Europe gathering impressions for paintings that have been shown throughout Denmark, Germany, Switzerland, and the United States. He served as the first president of the Copenhagen Stake.

Wayne C. Booth is George M. Pullman Professor of English at the University of Chicago. His books include *The Rhetoric of Fiction, Now Don't Try to Reason with Me, A Rhetoric of Irony,* and *Modern Dogma and the Rhetoric of Assent,* and he has edited *The Knowledge Most Worth Having.* He won the Christian Gauss Award (Phi Beta Kappa) in 1962 and the David H. Russel Award for Distinguished Research (National Council of Teachers of English) in 1966 for *The Rhetoric of Fiction* and is the recipient of the Brigham Young University College of Humanities Distinguished Alumnus Award.

Merrill Bradshaw studied music at Brigham Young University and the University of Illinois and joined the BYU faculty in 1957. He is a prolific composer whose music has delighted audiences throughout the world. Among his most recent works is his oratorio, *The Restoration.*

154

Yoshie Akimoto Eldredge began her piano studies in her native Japan and then continued them under James Friskin and Sasha Gorodnitski at the Juilliard School of Music. She has concertized widely in the United States and Japan. She now lives in Los Angeles and divides her time between performance, teaching, and family and church activities.

Herbert Harker, a Canadian by birth, is the author of two novels published by Random House: *Goldenrod* (1972) and *Turn Again Home* (1977). A Book-of-the-Month-Club alternate selection, *Goldenrod* was acclaimed in the *New York Times Book Review* as "one of the most enchanting novels ever written" and has been presented as a highly successful television special.

Edward L. Hart, a Utahn, received his doctorate from Oxford University and is currently professor of English at Brigham Young University. His major area of scholarly interest is English literature of the eighteenth century. His edition of biographies from the writings of John Nichols, *Minor Lives,* was published by Harvard University Press. In addition to many scholarly articles, he has also recently published a biographical study, *Mormon in Motion,* and a volume of poetry, *To Utah.*

Ruth Hoen, a native German, was for many years a leading soprano with the Cologne Opera. In addition to opera, she has had a successful career as a recitalist and has had a particular interest in the performance of sacred music, ranging from directing choirs in performance of hymns to singing solo parts in masses and oratorios. While serving as stake Relief Society president, she has been active in opera management.

Jon Carroll Lloyd is chief of surgery at Shadyside Hospital, Pittsburgh, Pennsylvania, and is associated with the Department of Surgery and the Program in Comparative Literature at the University of Pittsburgh. He is particularly respected for his development and advocacy of a program to teach the humanistic basis of therapeutics.

Karen Lynn was born and reared in southern California and received her Ph.D. from the University of Southern California. She has had postdoctoral research fellowships at Cambridge University and the University of Chicago. Among her research interests are medieval English literature, computer-assisted approaches to literary analysis, and twentieth-century values structures. She is associate professor of English at Brigham Young University.

Reid Nibley has been a member of the BYU faculty since 1969. As a concert pianist he has performed with various symphony orchestras and has made recordings that have received national acclaim. Dr. Nibley frequently performs with chamber groups and is a respected and much appreciated teacher.

Richard G. Oman has done graduate work at the University of Washington and worked at the Seattle Art Museum. He is currently manager of Museums and Artifacts for the Arts and Sites Division of the Church Historical Department. His special research interests are tribal art and the history and development of Mormon art.

Elder Boyd K. Packer, a native of Brigham City, Utah, was sustained an Assistant to the Quorum of the Twelve Apostles 3 October 1969 and was ordained an Apostle 2 December 1971. While serving as a General Authority he has been interested in the role and significance of the arts in the Church.

Candadai Seshachari was born in Hyderabad, India. He was the recipient of Fullbright and Danforth fellowships and is the author of *Ghandi and the American Scene: An Intellectual History and Inquiry.* He is currently director of general education and professor of English at Weber State College, Ogden, Utah.

Nicolas Shumway is a member of the Spanish faculty at Yale University, where he is departmental director of undergraduate education. He received his Ph.D. at UCLA and has pursued research in modern Spanish literature and various aspects of contemporary literary theory. He is the author of several studies that have appeared in leading journals, and he has sung professionally, appearing in the United States and Europe.

Trevor Southey, a Rhodesian by birth, began winning awards for his drawings as a child. He studied art in England, South Africa, and at Brigham Young University, where he was later a member of the art faculty for several years. In recent years he has devoted himself full-time to art. His paintings and sculptures have been shown throughout the United States.

Debra Sowell began her dance training as a child and has experience in many fields relating to dance. She has completed a graduate degree in the history of theater at Tufts University and has done extensive research on the recreation of renaissance court dances. She is a perceptive dance critic and historian and a welcome lecturer on various aspects of dance at Brigham Young University.

Anselm Spring is a man of extremely diversified accomplishments. A native of Germany, he has made an LP recording of his original songs and composes the music that accompanies his slide presentations. His photographs have appeared in several important European periodicals, and he is completing several book-length photographic essays.

Ishmael W. Stagner, II, has long been involved with and deeply committed to Hawaiian culture. He received much of his training in that culture from his mother, Pansy Kaulaleilehua Akona, and was awarded an Ed.D. degree by Brigham Young University. He is currently assistant professor of education and religion at Brigham Young University–Hawaii Campus.

Johann Wondra received a doctorate in theatric and cinematic arts from the University of Vienna. He is general secretary of the Vienna Burgtheater, perhaps the most venerable and respected theater in the German-speaking world. He has served as a branch president, in several mission presidencies, and is currently president of the Vienna Stake.